# Healthcare Finance:
# A Primer

## First Edition

BY

DEBORAH GORDON, ESQUIRE
STEPHEN J. BROWN, ESQUIRE

AMERICAN
**HEALTH LAWYERS**
ASSOCIATION

## RECENT TITLES FROM HEALTH LAWYERS

**Health Plans Contracting Handbook: A Guide for Payors and Providers, Fifth Edition**
© 2008, perfect bound

**Stark Final Regulations: A Comprehensive Analysis of Key Issues and Practical Guide, Fourth Edition**
© 2008, perfect bound

**Peer Review Hearing Guidebook, First Edition with CD-ROM**
© 2008, perfect bound

**The Complete "Connected" Pharmaceutical and Medical Devices Laws & Regulations**
© 2008, CD-ROM

**Clinical Research Practice Guide with CD-ROM**
© 2008, perfect bound

**Guide to Healthcare Legal Forms, Agreements, and Policies with CD-ROM**
© 2008, looseleaf

**False Claims Act & The Healthcare Industry: Counseling & Litigation, Second Edition**
© 2008, casebound

**Stark Phase III Guidance Collection**
© 2008, PDF

**Fundamentals of Health Law with CD-ROM, Fourth Edition**
© 2008, perfect bound

**AHLA's Federal Healthcare Laws & Regulations, 2007-2008 Edition**
© 2008, perfect bound 3-volume set

**Legal Issues in Healthcare Fraud and Abuse: Navigating the Uncertainties, 2007 Supplement**
© 2007, perfect bound

**Ambulatory Surgery Centers: CMS Update on Payment and Coverage**
© 2007, PDF

**The Complete "Connected" Civil False Claims Act Laws and Cases**
© 2007, CD-ROM

**Telemedicine: Survey and Analysis of Federal and State Laws with CD-ROM**
© 2007, perfect bound

**Healthcare Entity Bylaws with CD-ROM**
© 2007, perfect bound

**The Fundamentals of Life Sciences Law: Drugs, Devices, and Biotech with CD-ROM**
© 2007, perfect bound

**Institutional Review Boards: A Primer**
© 2007, perfect bound

**Fifty State Survey of Balance Billing Laws**
© 2007, perfect bound

# Preface

In 2007, Americans spent $2.3 trillion on healthcare, which amounts to 16% of the Country's gross domestic product. While the healthcare industry's significant cash flow and potential for future growth might lead one to assume that lenders would be eager to be involved, they remain reluctant, and healthcare finance, both debt and equity, remain highly specialized. For those involved with the healthcare industry, an understanding of the underlying principles of healthcare finance is a must.

Health Lawyers is pleased to bring you the first edition of *Healthcare Finance: A Primer*, and wants to express its tremendous gratitude to Deborah Gordon, Esquire, and Stephen J. Brown, Esquire, for authoring this new monograph. The authors address the ins and outs of healthcare finance, and cover all of the basics-from a discussion of the critical importance of finance to the future of healthcare to specific prototypical financial deals and the attending documents that accompany such deals.

The authors begin with an overview of the major issues that affect the financial aspects of healthcare: the aging population and its impact, costs associated with technological and scientific advances, and the need to address aging healthcare facilities and their capital improvement needs. They discuss the legal and economic issues addressed in specific federal laws, and note the need for lenders to understand how healthcare services are paid for and regulated in order to be able to both manage credit and risk as well as achieve consistent returns on their institutions' money. The authors delineate specific financial needs of specific types of healthcare entities, including hospitals, long term care facilities, life sciences companies, and numerous others.

Of critical importance in this area of the law is a basic understanding of the myriad options for financing, and the potential implications for each. Whether an institution chooses cash flow, asset-based, real estate or another method of financing, this publication addresses the concepts and documents most relevant to healthcare finance, including term sheets, due diligence, necessary legal opinions, pledge agreements, loan provisions, as well as what occurs in the event of a default and the post-default ramifications for the institutions. The authors examine four specific types of financing deals and discuss the relevant documents to each, and conclude with a discussion of potential credit enhancement methods and sources for financial institutions to reduce their risk potential. Finally, the authors have included valuable supplementary materials including a sample opinion for long term care facilities for a real estate loan, a sample asset-based opinion, and sample representations and warranties for life sciences companies.

We believe that the *Healthcare Finance: A Primer* will allow practitioners to identify and position their clients to respond to these issues in the years to come.

# About the Authors

**Deborah Gordon, Esquire,** is a partner at the law firm of Seyfarth Shaw LLP. Ms. Gordon concentrates her practice in the financial, corporate, and healthcare industries. Ms. Gordon regularly structures various types of business transactions, such as mergers and acquisitions, joint ventures, asset-based loans, cash flow loans, real estate financing transactions, mezzanine financing, convertible security issuances, leveraged buyouts, private placements, and private equity and venture capital transactions. She also has experience in secondary market transactions, including syndications and participations, and workouts, restructurings, and bankruptcies involving healthcare providers. Ms. Gordon regularly advises clients in the areas of healthcare regulatory matters, including licensing, fraud and abuse, privacy, medical staff issues, pharmaceutical pricing and marketing practices, compliance, and corporate governance. Ms. Gordon holds a J.D and a B.A. from the University of Illinois and an M.B.A. from the University of Chicago. She is a member of the Illinois Bar and has earned her Green Belt certificate in the firm's Six Sigma program.

**Stephen J. Brown, Esquire,** is an associate at the law firm of Seyfarth Shaw LLP. Mr. Brown focuses his practice primarily on commercial finance with secondary expertise in banking litigation, bankruptcy, insolvency, debt restructurings, workouts and the Uniform Commercial Code. He served as in-house counsel to a major mid-western bank for part of his career and during that time participated in the workout and restructuring of various healthcare related loans. Mr. Brown holds both a J.D. and an M.B.A in finance from the University of Wisconsin and a B.A. from the University of Minnesota. He is a member of the Wisconsin and Illinois Bars as well as the Illinois State Bar Association.

# Acknowledgements

The authors would like to thank the following contributing authors for their thoughtful insights and efforts: Tyler VanLonkhuyzen, James Schraidt, Andrew Lampert, and Nathan Coco. The authors would also like to thank Gabrielle Lewis for her research and assistance in putting this monograph together.

HEALTHCARE FINANCE:
A PRIMER

# Table of Contents

# 1

# Introduction and a View Forward

In 2007, Americans spent $2.3 trillion[1] on healthcare, representing 16% of the United States' gross domestic product (the GDP)[2]. The amount spent on healthcare has increased over 6% annually since 2001, far exceeding the rate of inflation.[3] A recent government report forecasts that the amount Americans spend on healthcare will climb to $4.3 trillion by 2017, which represents nearly 20% of projected GDP.[4] While some Americans may seek healthcare in other countries due to rising costs here, as a general matter, the off-shoring of medical goods and services is unlikely to alter this forecast in any material respect.

From a demographic perspective, the aging of 78 million baby boomers[5] is beginning to contribute to the rising healthcare needs of the U.S. population, and that trend will accelerate with each passing year. According to the U.S. Census Bureau, the population aged 65 and over is projected to grow 36% between 2010 and 2020 compared with an overall population growth rate of 9%. As a result, Americans should expect political and legal change relating to healthcare in response to this growth.

Significant healthcare reforms have already been proposed in the presidential election of 2008. The American electorate is responding to such proposals. Based on a Gallup poll, American voters consistently list healthcare reform as one of the top political issues that most directly affect them.[6]

Regardless of the outcome of the 2008 election, the issue of healthcare reform will be addressed in some manner. Republicans favor changes to tax policy and the implementation of new cost-cutting measures. Democrats propose a more substantial overhaul of the healthcare delivery system. Even in its most diluted form, any new healthcare plan would result in the most significant changes to the

---

[1] National Coalition on Healthcare, *Facts on the Cost of Health Care* http://www.nchc.org/facts/cost.shtml (last visited Apr. 21, 2008).
[2] *Id.* The Center for Medicare and Medicaid Services projects this percentage to increase by 1% every three years.
[3] U.S. Department of Health and Human Services, Centers for Medicare and Medicaid Services: *National Health Expenditure Data,* http://www.cms.hhs.gov/NationalHealthExpendData/25_NHE_Fact_Sheet.asp (last visited Apr. 21, 2008). *Health Care Costs Growing Faster than Inflation,* Health News, June 21, 2005, available at http://health.dailynewscentral.com/content/view/0001104/39/. National Coalition on Healthcare, *supra* note 1.
[4] Jane Zhang, *Medicare Spending to Surge,* Wall Street Journal, Feb. 26, 2008, at A3. *See also* The Centers for Medicare and Medicaid Services, "National Health Expenditure Projections 2007-2017," http://www.cms.hhs.gov/NationalHealthExpendData/03_NationalHealthAccountsProjected.asp#TopOfPage (last visited May 5, 2008).
[5] U.S. Census Bureau, (Baby boomers are people born in the post-World War II period from 1946 through 1964 and are estimated to consist of up to 26% of the population.), *Oldest Baby Boomer Turns 60,* (Jan. 3, 2006), available at http://www.census.gov/Press-Release/www/releases/archives/facts_for_features_special_editions/006105.html.
[6] PricewaterhouseCoopers, *Beyond the Sound Bite,* based upon PwC Health Research Institute a Bureau Economic Analysis, *Personal Consumption Components* (2007), available at https://pwc.com/extweb/home.nsf/docid/32E963D76D9414FD852573F3005CE7AA/$file/view-vol7-feature-health-print.html.

healthcare industry since 1965. Nationwide, approximately 47 million people, or approximately 15% of the population, are currently uninsured[7] and even the most conservative versions of the proposals would result in millions more people entitled to healthcare benefits. Immigration creates another large pool of new healthcare consumers. Finally, birth rates within the United States continue to be relatively high by developed country standards. Each of these factors contributes to likely increases in national healthcare expenditures. These increases will likely be paid for by some combination of mandatory and voluntary healthcare insurance purchases and increased taxation of upper-income Americans.

Considering the healthcare industry's significant cash flow and vast potential for growth, it is surprising, at least to the uninitiated, that many lenders express reluctance towards the healthcare industry. One would expect to see a stampede of the nation's financial institutions into the healthcare finance arena. As one pundit has put it, "It's the largest sector of the largest economy in the history of the world."[8] While $2 trillion is spent annually on healthcare, the aggregate number of loans syndicated by the nation's three largest healthcare finance companies during the period between September 1, 2006 and April 9, 2007 was less than $64 billion in the aggregate.[9]

Healthcare finance (both debt and equity) is highly specialized. The market swings back and forth like a pendulum, with new investors entering the field just as others exit. Sustained market momentum is illusive. For example, the Balanced Budget Act of 1997 dramatically changed the Medicare reimbursement formula for skilled nursing facilities, resulting in diminished revenues. This reimbursement reduction occurred at the same time plaintiff's attorneys focused their attention toward long term care facilities, resulting in increased costs.[10] As a result, many nursing homes struggled and lenders suffered. Integrated Health Services Inc., Mariner Health Care, Inc., and other large nursing-home chains sought bankruptcy protection or liquidation. This crisis coincided with the bankruptcy filing of Allegheny Health and Education and Research Foundation (AHERF) in Philadelphia, a large, nationally known medical center. Because of its size and notoriety, AHERF's bankruptcy filing affected the capital markets' assessment of healthcare credit risk.

Over the past few years, however, the industry has seen stable reimbursement and the pendulum has once again swung in favor of increased demand and higher occupancy rates. Some large banks and financial institutions have maintained fully specialized healthcare units for many years, but others have either not entered the healthcare marketplace or are just now beginning to realize the need for a healthcare unit. Meanwhile, smaller and mid-sized regional banks generally do not have stand-alone healthcare units.

Many lenders are reluctant to embrace the healthcare industry for a number of reasons. First, with a few notable exceptions such as certain developed and approved pharmaceutical products, the

---

[7] U.S. Census Bureau, *supra* note 5.

[8] Jessica Zigmond, *Going Strong, Going Public*, Modern Healthcare, Dec. 24, 2007, at 6. Quoting Ben Rooks, VP of Healthcare Investment Banking at William Blair.

[9] Thomson Financial, *By The Numbers: Largest Healthcare Financing Companies*, Modern Healthcare, May 21, 2007, at 46.

[10] Larry Reibstein, *Nursing-Home Verdicts: There's Guilt All Round*, Newsweek, July 27, 1998, at 34 (in one case, a jury awarded $83 million to the estate of a Texas resident who died of an untreated bedsore; the claim was later reduced to $55 million).

healthcare industry itself is a surprisingly low-margin affair, in large part because the industry gener- ally cannot, in its present form, control its costs.[11] Second, even during good times, the healthcare industry involves a host of regulatory complexities and uncertainty. The healthcare-generated assets that a financier might purchase, securitize, or lend against are often difficult for traditional bankers or underwriters to understand and evaluate.[12] Third, the industry is in a constant state of reform and, as a result, investors may be waiting for a legal or political catharsis before entering the market. These factors tend to reinforce each other, thereby inhibiting the growth of the healthcare finance industry.

During good economic times, lenders and finance companies often focus on opportunities in less regulated, easier to underwrite transactions. With sufficient demand for capital from other, more stable industries and consumers, lenders may experience sufficient deal flow without any need to delve into more complicated industries like healthcare. However, as economic times change, many lenders feel the pain of poor economic conditions, just as their borrowers do. The mortgage and real estate crisis of 2007 and 2008 has had a dramatic effect on consumers and financial institutions alike.

Despite the hesitancy felt by lenders, many economists consider the healthcare industry to be recession resistant, under the theory that medically necessary services are in demand regardless of economic circumstances. Similarly, pharmaceutical or biotechnology companies with critical care products may be less vulnerable to economic slowdowns. On the other hand, there are other segments of the healthcare industry that may be impacted by a slow economy. For instance, preventive care and health maintenance services generally are negatively affected with increased unemployment, loss of medical coverage, and higher co-pays and deductibles. Moreover, elective procedures may decline along with reduced consumer confidence and increased unemployment rates.

There also are some instances in which negative economic news may benefit certain healthcare sectors and damage others. A drop in the housing market, for example, could result in fewer senior citizens entering into independent living or assisted living communities because they cannot sell their residences. The loss to the independent living and assisted living communities, however, could prove to be a benefit for home health providers.

---

[11] Pricewaterhouse Coopers' Health Research Institute released a report in 2008 entitled "The Price of Excess," in which it estimated wasteful spending in the healthcare system to be $1.2 trillion of the $2.2 trillion spent nationally, more than one half of all healthcare spending. The report identifies the top three areas of wasted spending to be defensive medicine, inefficient claims processing, and care spent on preventable conditions related to obesity. Similarly, rising levels of bad debt expenses and costs related to uncompensated care affect the revenue levels of many healthcare providers.

[12] *See generally*, Seth Lubove, *As a financier of last resort to the health care industry, National Century Financial Enter- prises has made its owners rich, but not without controversy*, Forbes.com, Oct. 28, 2002, at http://www.forbes.com/ forbes/2002/1028/150.html:

> The high profile collapse of National Century Financial Enterprises (NCFE) in 2002 contributed to some lenders' reluctance to lend against healthcare collateral. NCFE lent money to healthcare providers, primarily secured by governmental receivables. Since federal programs are often slow to pay, certain healthcare facilities needed to access capital secured by those payments for cash flow needs. NCFE purchased accounts receivable from health- care providers. NCFE then raised capital secured by those accounts receivables. However, the receivables were not as robust as represented. Similarly, many payors would not pay NCFE directly, instead paying the healthcare facilities.

A fundamental understanding of these economic and sociopolitical factors issues is important for borrowers, lenders, and their respective lawyers. While a thorough analysis of the driving changes in the healthcare industry is beyond the scope of this monograph, this monograph highlights some of the major socioeconomic issues affecting the healthcare industry. This monograph also discusses the capital needs of various components of the healthcare industry and specific financing strategies to meet these capital needs.

## 1.1  Healthcare Finance is More Important than Ever

The healthcare industry's need for capital is growing dramatically and will likely continue to do so in the coming decades. Consequently, both the financial institutions that are operating in the healthcare industry as well as those that have thus far avoided the healthcare sector will have plenty of additional lending and investment opportunities in the years to come. The following are some of the main reasons why healthcare is so capital intensive and why additional capital will be necessary.

### 1.1.1  Aging Population

The demand for medical services will increase sharply as more baby boomers reach ages at which they require increased medical care. As demand for healthcare products and services increases without a corresponding increase in supply, a commensurate rise in prices will occur unless sufficient capital investment is made that will eventually allow for increased supply.[13] A recent study suggests that capital accounts at the nation's hospitals are already underfunded by between 10 to 20 billion dollars in the aggregate because revenues must be spent on operations rather than capital improvements.[14] Due to the relatively small profit margins of the healthcare industry, it stands to reason that the majority of the investment necessary for expanding long-term healthcare supply to accommodate national demographics must come from new investors.

### 1.1.2  Longer Life Expectancy

Not only are the numbers of older Americans increasing, but older Americans are living longer. Naturally, this allows consumers more time in which to consume healthcare products and services, which they may do at increasing rates as they reach the end of their longer lives.

---

[13] Grubb & Ellis, *Aging Baby Boomers Will Drive Demand for Healthcare Properties Over Next Decade*, Apr. 3, 2008, press release available at http://www.grubb-ellis.com/corpinfo/news_rel_detail.aspx?Article=525 (last visited May 1, 2008).

> Grubb & Ellis Company announced in a report dated April 3, 2008, that medical office space is already outperforming traditional office space as measured by asking rental rates. Similarly, the Grubb & Ellis report indicates that monthly spending on healthcare construction is 20% higher than a year ago. Four states accounted for one-third of healthcare starts in 2007: California, Florida, Texas and Illinois. In addition, according to the National Ambulatory Medicare Care Survey, individuals 65 to 74 made an average of 6.5 visits per capita physicians' offices in 2005 compared with 3.3 visits per capita for all age groups. The 75 and over age group made an average of 7.7 visits per capita. Meanwhile, the average number of visits per capital for all age groups increased from 2.7 in 1985 to 3.3 in 2005, suggesting a rising propensity among all consumers in general to access healthcare services.

[14] Jacqueline Palank, *Study: Thousands of Hospitals are on the Brink of Insolvency*, Daily Bankruptcy Review, Apr. 28, 2008, at 5 (citing a study by the restructuring firm of Alvarez & Marsal released in Apr. 2008).

### 1.1.3     Labor Shortages

Labor costs are the most significant component of any service industry. If one views labor as a global economic commodity whose price rises and falls with worldwide supply and demand, then one should expect that the cost of labor will increase in the coming years. The reason is that the size of the labor force serving the healthcare industry is not predicted to increase ratably with demand, in part because the retirement of the baby boomers will likely cancel out new sources of labor. But as the baby boomers retire and grow older, they will demand significantly more medical services. Further, a recent report by the federal Institute of Medicine states that the existing United States healthcare work is insufficiently trained in geriatric care for the baby boomer generation.[15] With more money and more patients demanding the services of roughly the same number of service providers (*i.e.*, laborers), labor costs are predicted to continue rising sharply in the coming decades. Moreover, the United States will not be the only country bidding up the price of labor, as other wealthy nations will face the same demographic challenges and the same labor shortages. Some analysts project that by 2025 there may be a shortage of as many as 500,000 nurses in the United States, which would create a vacancy rate of around 40%.[16] The wealthier nations already are luring professional medical service providers, especially veteran nurses, away from poorer nations, often leaving local patients underserved and causing international rancor.[17] As healthcare labor becomes an increasingly fungible international commodity, its price will continue to be bid up by the wealthier nations.

### 1.1.4     Defensive Medicine

Beyond proscribing illegal practices, the American legal system does not mandate or closely control how healthcare providers treat their patients. The tort system, however, allows for patients to sue for damages when they can prove that they were harmed by substandard care.

Tort lawyers look to and beyond the doctor's professional liability insurance policy to satisfy malpractice claims. The tort bar has argued that malpractice claims benefit society as a whole by holding healthcare providers responsible for their actions and that the cost of all tort judgments represents only a small percentage of overall health costs.[18] The bar also notes that malpractice losses have held steady for various years yet healthcare costs continue to rise.[19] Irrespective of one's political position regarding medical malpractice suits, there is no question that the proliferation of malpractice claims has increased—and continues to increase—the cost of medical malpractice insurance.

---

[15]  Theo Francis and Vanessa Fuhrmans, *Geriatric Care Is Facing Crisis: Surge in Training Called for to Meet Exploding Demand,* Wall Street Journal, Apr. 15, 2008, at D2.

[16]  Conor Dougherty, *Slowdown's Side Effect: More Nurses,* Wall Street Journal, May 7, 2008, at D1 (citing to "*The Future of the Nursing Workforce in the U.S.,*" by Peter Buerhaus, Douglas Staiger, and David Auerbach).

[17]  *See generally* Mireille Kingma, *Nurses on the Move: Migration and the Global Healthcare Economy*, Cornell University Press (2006).

[18]  Towers Perrin, *2007 Update on U.S. Tort Cost Trends,* 2007, at 9. (Medical malpractice costs have been estimated to be approximately $30.3 Billion).

[19]  Americans for Insurance Reform, Medical Malpractice Insurance: *Stable Losses/Unstable Rates 2007,* Mar. 28, 2007, available at http://www.centerjd.org/air/StableLosses2007.pdf (last visited May 2, 2008).

Aside from the directly measurable tort losses and increased insurance costs, the prevalence of malpractice claims causes many physicians to practice medicine in a defensive manner. Physicians undertake procedures designed to reduce or eliminate potential tort liability resulting in increased costs, such as ordering tests and other procedures that may not be necessary or cost-effective. By performing these tests or procedures, however, the medical provider may be protected from the small risk that, if such testing and procedures had not been performed, a medical problem leading to a tort claim might have arisen or might not have been identified. Although it is impossible to calculate the additional costs arising from the practice of defensive medicine, there is no doubt that the performance of millions of arguably unnecessary medical procedures and tests every year materially contributes to the high costs of healthcare.

While the tort system creates an incentive for medical providers to practice defensive medicine, the parties ultimately responsible for payment of medical costs (such as insurance companies, employers, union funds, Medicare, and Medicaid) are attempting to counteract this incentive by profiling providers and making credentialing and provider contracting decisions based upon utilization and efficiency. Consequently, healthcare providers are under pressure to control costs and over-utilization despite the counter pressure from plaintiff's attorneys to exhaust all diagnostic and treatment options.

In response to the conflicting pressures of the tort system and the parties paying for medical costs, healthcare providers increasingly are requiring patients to forfeit their right to sue the provider by inserting binding arbitration provisions in their standard contracts. While controversial, the use of binding arbitration has been successful and has reduced the average malpractice costs for nursing homes.[20]

### 1.1.5    Technological and Scientific Advances

Advances in medicine and technology also have resulted in increased demand for services on a per capita basis, particularly advances that result in new or safer procedures. For example, when gastric bypass surgery was first introduced, many payors did not cover the procedure since it was deemed to be medically unnecessary. However, as gastric bypass surgery has been shown to reduce the incidence of many obesity related diseases and health problems, many payors now see the surgery as cost-effective from an overall health perspective.[21]

The cost of developing new medicine and technology is high and must be priced into every unit sold or test performed. With life on the line, however, cost becomes less important. Moreover, expensive lifesaving treatments may not, in many cases, be denied persons who cannot pay for them. These costs also must be priced into products and services sold to those who can pay. As a result, newly developed medical procedures, devices or drugs are often expensive for medical providers, patients, and third party payors.

---

[20] Nathan Koppel, *Nursing Homes, in Bid to Cut Costs, Prod Patients to Forgo Lawsuits,* Wall Street Journal, includes a study by Aon Global Risk consulting, Apr. 11, 2008, at A1.

[21] Medicare Advisory Payment Committee (MedPac), *Report to the Congress: Promoting Greater Efficiency in Medicare,* June 2007, at 9. Approximately one-fourth of Medicare spending was attributed to obese beneficiaries in 2002.

Finally, hospitals often feel pressure to purchase new equipment even if the equipment may not be necessary or may only contribute marginally to the level of care provided. This pressure arises from marketing concerns, among other things, and the need to have the latest equipment to attract the best doctors and therefore, the most patients.

### 1.1.6  Aging Healthcare Facilities and Capital Improvement Needs

Hospital and health facility construction and capital improvement costs are rising. In addition to aging and outdated facilities, construction and capital improvement needs arise from the shift to outpatient care, increased patient volume, technological advances, and increased competition. Technology acquisitions include purchases of digital radiology equipment, computerized medical record systems, and other information technology systems. Increases in capacity often involve new or expanded outpatient centers, increased emergency room and operating room capacity, and patient room renovations. In addition, hospitals and healthcare facilities are investing in more energy-efficient materials and architectural designs.

Nursing homes, in particular, are in need of outside capital. The median age of nursing homes is 29 years, and nearly 33% of skilled nursing facilities are in need of improvement.[22] With respect to hospitals, a Healthcare Financial Management Association study from 2006 showed that 72% of hospital and healthcare system CFOs project that their capital spending will increase by an average of 14% within the next five years. Similarly, 85% of hospital CFOs indicated that it will become more difficult to fund capital expenditures in the future.

## 1.2  Cost of Capital

As with any other business, the healthcare industry's ability to use money is limited by the costs that it must pay for that use, *i.e.*, its cost of capital. In the case of debt, the cost of capital consists of the fees and interest payable on a loan and is based upon the amount of risk that a lender perceives in making the applicable loan. With equity, the cost of capital is derived from the risk perceived by the investors. If a risk-to-reward ratio is high, the investors will either require a greater return on their investment or invest their money elsewhere. Accordingly, if a business is perceived as risky, the cost of capital, whether it is obtained through debt or equity financing, will be higher. This high cost of capital creates a potential barrier to entry into the healthcare industry and can stifle competition.

The healthcare industry historically has been plagued by a high cost of capital, because it is generally perceived as risky, complicated, and underperforming. As a result, the private sector is often unwilling to invest a relatively high percentage of the funds necessary to support the industry, which means that a greater burden falls upon the public sector and healthcare providers for financing needs. For example, hospitals may divert non-core assets, look to more joint ventures, or elect to self-fund insurance to address their capital needs. In addition, many healthcare providers have moved medical office buildings or other non-core assets off their balance sheets to generate cash and enhance debt capacity. Some specialized real estate investment trusts (REITs) purchase healthcare properties and then lease the real estate back to the operator.

---

[22] *See generally* National Investment Center, *NIC Market Area Profiles,* http://www.nic.org/ (last visited May 1, 2008).

If the cost of capital to healthcare providers was lower, providers would be more profitable because they would be able to retain their core and non-core assets. The dollars used to pay the costs of capital could either be retained or invested elsewhere in the industry. This increase in profitability would spark the interest of the private sector, which would be more willing to contribute to the financing of the healthcare industry and, consequently, would reduce the strain on the public sector.

### 1.2.1    Role of Government

The federal government plays an important role in contributing to the healthcare industry's cost of capital. In 2005, the federal government paid almost a trillion dollars in healthcare costs, which represented approximately 47% of all healthcare expenditures in the United States.[23] As described later in this monograph, however, laws and regulations complicate the collateral assignment of government receivables and the ability of lenders to realize on what should be a ready source of collateral. As a result of these complications, healthcare providers are less able to leverage their most significant assets when borrowing funds in the debt markets.

Healthcare providers also are subject to the unpredictable and somewhat arbitrary manner in which the government reimburses them for services provided. The Center for Medicare and Medicaid Services (CMS) frequently adjusts reimbursement amounts, often resulting in drastic payment cuts. The ambiguity and uncertainty of the reimbursement process makes it difficult for healthcare providers to accurately project cash flow. If their revenue streams were more predictable, loans to healthcare providers would be inherently less risky. By simplifying receivable assignment rules and taking actions to increase cash flow predictability, the government could lower the healthcare industry's cost of capital.

### 1.2.2    Role of Finance Providers

Lenders also have a major role to play in the reduction of capital costs in the healthcare industry. For decades, commercial banks have made ad hoc loans to healthcare providers. The mortgage loans are often treated as typical real estate transactions, and the cash flow and asset-based loans often have been divided among banking groups based upon whether the borrower was a for-profit or not-for-profit entity—their identical products and similar operations notwithstanding. Moreover, banks historically have organized their origination units geographically rather than by fields of expertise. As a result, many individual bankers and their groups are not able to specialize in particular fields, and any institutional healthcare expertise that exists remains fractured and undeveloped. This lack of institutional expertise perpetuates the financial sector's perception of risk in the healthcare industry because many bankers lack a complete understanding of the business.

Many parties in the financial sector are realizing, however, that they need to develop expertise in the healthcare arena in order to remain competitive. Again, the healthcare industry currently represents approximately 16% of the GNP, and that percentage is rising.[24] As a result, many major banks have

---

[23] Ricardo Alonso-Zaldivar, *National Healthcare Costs Topped $2 Trillion in 2006*, Los Angeles Times, Jan. 8, 2008, at A8.

[24] National Coalition on Healthcare, *Facts on the Cost of Health Care*, available at http://www.nchc.org/facts/cost.shtml (last visited May 1, 2008).

developed either internal units that are dedicated solely to the healthcare industry or multidisciplinary teams that cooperate with one another in the origination of healthcare-related loan and investment products.

As more lenders develop expertise in the healthcare industry, they will be better able to manage the risk of their healthcare portfolios. For example, the increased lender concentration in this sector should lead to increased opportunities to syndicate larger loans among several financial institutions and to sell them into the capital markets.

Another potential growth area for healthcare finance is demand side financing. If third party payors balk at paying for advanced or elective procedures, insured, and private-pay patients may need short-term loans for surgeries or other major healthcare expenses. This phenomenon already is occurring in Great Britain, where citizens increasingly seek private financing for costly drugs and procedures that the government's universal care system refuses to cover.[25] Demand side financing also has become available in the United States in the context of elective surgeries, where, for example, ambulatory surgical centers offer various financing "plans" for knee and hip surgeries underwritten by a commercial bank.

## 1.3    Likely Effects of Future Healthcare Reform on Healthcare Finance

### 1.3.1    Healthcare Reform

Given the potentially significant changes in the regulation of the healthcare industry, some financial institutions might believe it makes sense to wait until matters settle before forging ahead into the marketplace. The changes currently proposed vary in many respects, and they are mere starting points in an intense political negotiation that should last for many years.

Nevertheless, by looking closely at the current proposed reforms and then making some reasonably safe assumptions as to how each might evolve in political negotiation, it is possible to develop a fairly good understanding of how and why healthcare could change in the coming decades.

In analyzing the future of healthcare, it is instructive to review its recent history. In 1993, a Clinton administration initiative, headed by Hillary Clinton, proposed a sweeping overhaul of the federal healthcare regime to Congress. The proposal focused, among other things, on mandated employer insurance coverage and a large federal bureaucracy to enforce the law. This proposal failed.

The first lesson from the failure of the Clinton administration's proposal was that it is not possible to pass sweeping transformative reforms that destroy or render obsolete many of the institutions with vested interests in the American healthcare system. Another lesson learned is that it is not practical to try to do too much in any one law. The federal healthcare regime is too complex and there are too many special interests to accomplish immediate change. Rather, reform must take an evolutionary and bipartisan form and must account for both the old players and the new players in the industry.

---

[25] *See, e.g.*, Graham Satchell, *I Have Been Denied Vital Cancer Drug*, BBC News, Jan. 31, 2008, available at http://news.bbc.co.uk/go/pr/fr/-/2/hi/health/7219373.stm.

### 1.3.2    Demand Side Analysis

Because reform in the healthcare system tends to be evolutionary, it is unlikely that the government will institute a Canadian or European-styled single-source payor system. Instead, the government likely will implement a number of strategies whereby governmental authorities at the federal and state levels will intervene to assist the uninsured in procuring insurance from private vendors. The result over time should be greatly increased demand for healthcare products and services.

Currently, states are attempting to close the uninsured gap by legally mandating that private insurance policies sold in such states cover an ever-increasing list of medical problems and procedures. In addition, since 2005, 31 states have enacted laws requiring employers satisfying certain criteria to maintain health insurance for their employees or to otherwise compensate their employees. In Massachusetts, for example, employers with at least 10 employees that do not contribute to any employee's health coverage must pay each such employee $295 annually. In July 2006, the City of San Francisco passed a Healthcare Security Ordinance mandating that for-profit businesses with 20 or more employees and non-profit businesses with 50 or more employees pay healthcare benefits for employees satisfying certain criteria. The ordinance became effective in January 2008 and has survived initial challenges in federal courts. It is reasonably likely that piecemeal laws and ordinances such as these, as well as other demand side changes, will continue to occur in the future.

### 1.3.3    Supply Side Analysis

Demand side questions focus on how much will be spent on healthcare and who will pay. Supply side questions, on the other hand, relate to who will supply healthcare services, what quantities will be provided, and how such "services" will be defined. Here as well, dramatic changes are in the offing, which tend to increase the types and classes of healthcare providers that require financing. Healthcare supply should therefore expand not just because of larger demand-side expenditure but also because of an expanding definition of what "healthcare" is.

The traditional paradigm of the delivery of healthcare services has shifted. In the past, the healthcare provider, often a doctor, dictated the course of treatment. Now, however, patients are more likely to take greater control of their own medical care. In part, greater patient involvement and control is caused by the greater financial responsibility placed on patients by the relative decline of employer-provided healthcare insurance. Patients who pay more of the bill are less inclined to be passive consumers. Third party payors also play an increased role in directing healthcare spending.

As an initial matter, healthcare providers are providing new and different services than they once did because providers, payors, and individual patients have all realized in varying degrees that healthcare should focus more on prevention and maintenance than on treatment. In the past, diet, exercise, and "therapy" of various types were often ignored because the healthcare system was reactive. People went to the doctor when there was something wrong with them. Now, some larger employers pay for nutrition education, gym memberships, and anti-smoking programs because they believe that these cash outlays will save money in the long run. These new attitudes are also economic harbingers. Indeed, the proactive "health management" sector, as opposed to the reactive disease treatment sector, is now one of the most rapidly growing new healthcare suppliers.

As patients and payors have taken greater control over healthcare consumption, they have increased their demands for greater transparency. Quantitative and qualitative information with respect to pricing and the actual quality of the services performed is now at a premium. "Transparency" has become a marketing weapon used by some providers to tout their product. The patient today increasingly views herself as a consumer in a world filled with service providers that must compete for her business.

As the supply side continues to expand and fracture, competition should increase, not just among traditional providers, but between competing concepts of what healthcare means. Laser eye surgery is often used as an example of the alleged benefits of competition, deregulation, greater transparency, and a break with the traditional doctor-dominated supply chain. The laser eye surgical industry has been criticized by ophthalmologists as "the corporatization of medicine in the most extreme form."[26] Because laser surgery is considered non-invasive, many state professional licensing agencies allow non-physicians, such as optometrists, to perform it. Since the procedure is considered cosmetic, many insurance companies, at least initially, refused to cover it. Consequently, the surgery was traditionally paid for directly by the consumer.

The result was the rapid "commoditization" of eye surgery, the creation of a specialized industry, and a drastic increase in the number of eye surgeries performed. The cost for the procedure plummeted as supply increased.

---

[26] Milt Freudenheim, *Turning Surgery Into a Commodity; Laser Eye Centers Wage an All-Out Price War*, New York Times, Dec. 9, 2000, at C1.

# 2

# Legal and Economic Issues in Healthcare Lending

## 2.1    Beyond Mere Money

To state the obvious, a loan to a hospital used, in part, to treat patients is different from a loan to, say, a car manufacturer. The nature of the healthcare "product" raises moral and ethical issues to which even the most hardened capitalist is sensitive. While cynics may blithely state that moral considerations do not matter to capitalist institutions, many people who work for banks will say that they do, if for no other reason than to avoid public relations disasters. These special issues cause the finance community to view healthcare finance transactions as a breed apart.

## 2.2    Healthcare Laws

In order to manage credit risk and achieve consistent returns in the healthcare industry, lenders must understand how healthcare services are paid for and regulated. Prior to the development of traditional healthcare insurance coverage, the most common form of healthcare insurance was indemnity healthcare insurance. Indemnity insurance is similar to life insurance in that an insurance company charges a healthcare insurance premium, invests the premium dollars, and uses the premium dollars and the earnings to pay out prospective healthcare claims. In the past, advances in healthcare technology were relatively slow and malpractice awards were relatively small, so insurance companies were earning money on the invested premium dollars, and the indemnity-based insurance model provided a relatively stable mechanism for the healthcare industry. When healthcare costs began to rise and malpractice awards rose dramatically, premiums likewise rose and, eventually, traditional indemnity insurance companies could no longer continue to operate under this "prospective pay" model. Consequently, the concept of government-sponsored programs and managed care began to appear more attractive to those entities responsible for the payment of healthcare services.

### 2.2.1    Medicare and Medicaid

Medicare is a federal governmental health insurance system under which physicians, hospitals, and other healthcare providers are reimbursed or paid directly for services provided to eligible elderly and disabled persons. Medicare is administered by the Centers for Medicare and Medicaid Services, or CMS, of the federal Department of Health and Human Services. In order to achieve and maintain Medicare certification, healthcare providers must meet CMS's Conditions of Participation on an ongoing basis.

Medicare provides certain healthcare benefits to beneficiaries who are 65 years of age or older, blind, disabled or qualify for the End Stage Renal Disease Program. Medicare Part A covers inpatient hospital services, skilled nursing care and some home healthcare. By virtue of their eligibility for Social Security benefits, older Americans qualify for Medicare Part A, or the hospital insurance program. Medicare Part A is funded through payroll or FICA taxes.

Medicare Part B covers physician services and certain supplies. Medicare Part B is the supplemental medical insurance program and is a voluntary program. Persons eligible for Medicare Part A may enroll in Part B by paying a monthly premium. Medicare Part B covers services provided by healthcare professionals and suppliers, such as physician services, laboratory tests, and outpatient services.

Medicare Part C addresses the Medicare managed care program and Medicare Part D provides beneficiaries with prescription drug benefits.

Certain Medicare beneficiaries may choose to obtain their benefits through a variety of risk-based plans under Medicare Part C, or the Medicare Advantage Program, formerly known as the Medicare+Choice Program. The Medicare Advantage Program generally allows Medicare beneficiaries to participate in coordinated care plans, including health maintenance organizations (HMOs) and provider networks sponsored by hospitals, physicians, or other providers, fee-for-service plans that accept full capitation from the Medicare program, and medical savings account plans that allow certain seniors to enroll in a high deductible medical benefit plan. A healthcare provider may contract with CMS to provide Medicare Advantage services, either as a state-licensed HMO or as a provider-sponsored organization for which CMS has waived state-licensure requirements. All Medicare Advantage organizations must assume full financial risk on a prospective basis for the provision of health services.

Medicaid is a health insurance program for certain low-income and needy individuals which is jointly funded by the federal government and the individual states. Each state administers its own Medicaid program, establishes its own eligibility standards and determines the type, amount, duration, and scope of services. Each state also sets the payment rates for such services. The Medicaid program is funded through federal and state tax revenues. Medicaid covers a full range of healthcare services, such as inpatient and outpatient services, nursing facility services, physician services, and, in some cases, prescribed drugs. Each state pays for such services in accordance with procedures and standards established by state law pursuant to federal guidelines.

Because large amounts are paid by the government for healthcare services through Medicare, Medicaid, and other programs, laws dictating how and when the government will pay healthcare providers[1] are economically and legally important. In 2005, for example, the federal government's social security and Medicare programs paid out $845 billion dollars.[2] Collectively, federal, state, and local

---

[1] Medicare makes a distinction between healthcare *suppliers* and healthcare *providers*. In this monograph, those terms are used interchangeably and not in the technical senses set forth by Medicare law. Each refers simply to the universe of persons and institutions who provide healthcare services to the American public.

[2] Alan Greenspan, *The Age of Turbulence: Adventures in a New World*, at 419, Penguin Press (2007).

governments paid approximately 47% of the nation's total healthcare bill in 2005 to 2006.[3] Accordingly, any change in reimbursement policies often has a dramatic effect on the healthcare industry.

For example, Congress enacted the Balanced Budget Act in 1997, which dramatically cut reimbursement for skilled nursing facilities. The result was a significant increase in distressed nursing homes until the industry adapted. Now, nursing homes market their services to Medicare and private-pay patients requiring shorter stays for rehabilitation. Medicare generally only pays for skilled nursing rehabilitation services while Medicaid covers long-term stays in skilled nursing facilities. Since Medicaid reimbursement results in extremely low profit margins, many facilities focus on payor mix to achieve better margins.

A substantial portion of the Medicare revenues are derived from payments made for services rendered to Medicare beneficiaries under a variety of prospective payment systems (PPS). Under PPS, the amount paid to the provider for an episode or unit of care is established by federal regulation and is not directly related to the provider's charges or actual costs of providing that care. Inpatient, outpatient, rehabilitation and long-term care hospital services, skilled nursing care, and home healthcare are paid on the basis of PPS, with certain exceptions.[4] Under the Medicare hospital inpatient PPS, fixed payment amounts per inpatient discharge are established based on the patient's assigned diagnosis related group (DRG). DRGs classify treatments for illnesses according to the estimated intensity of hospital resources necessary to furnish care for each principal diagnosis.[5] All services paid under the Medicare hospital outpatient services are classified into groups called ambulatory payment classifications, or APCs. Services in each APC are similar clinically and in terms of the resources they require. A payment rate is established for each APC.

From time to time, the factors used in calculating the prospective payments for units of service are modified by CMS, which may increase or reduce revenues for particular services. The importance of these occasional changes, and the financial dislocation that they cause, is hard to overstate. The wrong change can cause a large and unforeseeable drop in revenue for a healthcare provider.

### 2.2.1.1 Hospitals

Currently, most hospitals receive a large percentage of their funds from patient revenues, and the largest portion of those revenues are paid by third party payors. In 2003, hospitals derived nearly 46% of their total funding, or $765.7 billion, from governmental sources, primarily Medicare and Medicaid.[6] Meanwhile, the remainder of hospital revenue, more than $913.2 billion, was derived from

---

[3] Ricardo Alonso-Zaldivar, *National Healthcare Costs Topped $2 Trillion in 2006*, Los Angeles Times, at A8.
[4] *See* 49 Fed. Reg. 234, Jan. 3, 1984. Those hospitals excluded by statute are: (i) psychiatric hospitals; (ii) rehabilitation hospitals; (iii) children's hospitals; (iv) long-term care hospitals; (v) distinct psychiatric and rehabilitation units; (vi) hospitals outside the 50 states; and (vii) hospitals in states with an approved waiver.
[5] Under the DRG payment system, all of the diagnoses from the Internal Classification of Diseases, 9th Revision, Clinical Modification (ICD9-CM) System are classified into 25 major diagnostic categories based on organ systems. These 25 categories are then broken down into 495 DRGs. Each DRG is then assigned a price established for 495 specific diagnostic categories, subject to certain modifiers. These prices are updated annually by Medicare to reflect inflationary changes as well as changes in treatment protocols.
[6] Centers for Medicare and Medicaid, *National Health Accounts: Definitions, Sources and Method Used in National Expenditures*, 2003, Aug. 20, 2005.

other third party payors.[7] There also are some non-patient revenues that come by way of government grants for research purposes or direct payments to subsidized hospitals, such as county facilities, but the majority of non-patient revenues come from tax support or other financing.

Under the DRG system, operating payments to hospitals are based upon the multiplication of (i) the hospital's dollar rate and (ii) the specific case value of a DRG. A specific value is assigned to each of the 495 DRGs, and a hospital's dollar rate depends on the hospital's designation as large, urban, or other. Each of the DRGs and the hospital's designations are defined once a year by Medicare. The periodic adjustments to DRGs can have disastrous consequences for hospitals because substantial capital investments have been made or are budgeted based upon prevailing reimbursement standards. The prospect of ever-changing reimbursement rules causes healthcare providers a great deal of financial uncertainty and distress.

Additional payments may be made to individual providers. Hospitals that treat a disproportionately large number of low-income patients currently receive additional payments in the form of disproportionate share payments (or DSH payments). Additional payments made to hospitals that treat patients who are costlier to treat than the average patient are called "outlier payments". Outlier payments are made in those cases in which a patient uses an unusually large amount of resources, which are based on the total cost of the applicable patient and the number of days the patient is in the hospital.[8] Eligible hospitals are paid for a portion of their direct and indirect medical education costs. Teaching hospitals, for example, are given additional payments based on the number of interns and residents at the hospital and the number of beds.

### 2.2.1.2    *Long-Term Care Facilities and Nursing Homes*

Medicare provides limited nursing home benefits, covering only post-hospitalization stays in skilled nursing facilities (SNFs).[9] SNFs are paid pursuant to the PPS and the payment rates are adjusted for case mix and geographic variation in wages.[10] Under the Balanced Budget Act, SNFs must use the PPS on a per-diem basis which is adjusted on a case-by-case basis using a resident classification system and factoring in geographic adjustments and annual updates.[11]

To be covered by Medicare, the patient must have been hospitalized for at least three days and must generally have entered the SNF within 30 days after hospital discharge.[12] Additionally, the services

---

[7]  *Id.*

[8]  42 C.F.R. §§ 412.80–.86.

[9]  Social Security Act §§ 1812(a)(2)(A), 1861(i), 42 U.S.C. §§ 1395d(a)(2)(A), 1395x; 42 C.F.R. §§ 409.20–.27; U.S. Department of Health & Human Services, Centers for Medicare & Medicaid Services, *Medicare Intermediary Manual*, Part 3 § 3131, available at http://www.cms.hhs.gov/manuals/pbm/ItemDetail.asp?ItemID=CMS021918 (last visited April 30, 2008). Medicare can, however, extend coverage to admissions that do not follow hospitalizations if it finds that such coverage would be budget-neutral. Social Security Act § 1812(a)(2)(B), (f), 42 U.S.C. § 1395d(a)(2)(B), (f).

[10]  CMS uses Resource Utilization Groups to help determine a daily payment rate for SNFs.

[11]  CMS is proposing a recalibration of these adjustments for fiscal year 2009.

[12]  U.S. Department of Health & Human Services, Centers for Medicare & Medicaid Services, *Glossary*, available at http://www.cms.hhs.gov/apps/glossary/ last visited May 2, 2008. (A spell of illness under Medicare is defined as a period of consecutive days, beginning with the first day on which a beneficiary is furnished inpatient hospital or extended care services, and ending with the close of the first period of sixty (60) consecutive days thereafter in which the beneficiary is in neither a hospital nor a skilled nursing facility.)

furnished by the SNF must either be related to the condition for which the patient was hospitalized or to a condition that developed while the patient was in the SNF. Finally, reimbursement for a SNF stay is contingent upon the following criteria being satisfied: (i) the patient must need skilled nursing care or skilled rehabilitation services; (ii) this need must exist on a daily basis; and (iii) as a practical matter, the patient's need can be satisfied only through inpatient care in a SNF.[13]

Even if Medicare covers a stay in a SNF, that stay is limited to 100 days during any single "spell of illness."[14] Additionally, patients are responsible for coinsurance equal to one-eighth of the daily hospital deductible for days 21 through 100 of a SNF stay.[15] Upon the expiration of the 100-day period, Medicare Part B coverage (*e.g.*, physician coverage) may still cover some of the SNF's services, such as X rays, laboratory and other diagnostic tests, surgical dressings, radiation therapy, prosthetics, prosthetic devices, orthotics, outpatient physical and occupational therapy, speech-language pathology services, and ambulance services.[16] Yet, even with this limited coverage, Medicare reimbursement for SNF care has increased from $0.3 billion in 1980 to $21 billion in 2007.[17] Still, given that Medicare's reimbursement for SNF stays are limited, the majority of patients are forced to pay for long-term or nursing care either out-of-pocket or though private insurance.

Medicaid, on the other hand, is the primary funding source for long-term care services. Medicaid spending on long-term care includes spending for institutional nursing facilities, intermediate care facilities (ICFs), and home and community care.

Medicaid spending almost doubled from 1991 to 1997, with an increase in the share devoted to home and community-based services and a decline in the share devoted to ICFs. This shift reflects, in part, greater state use of Medicaid waivers for home and community-based services.

### 2.2.1.3    Physicians and Other Providers/Suppliers

Medicare uses a fee schedule to pay physicians or other providers and suppliers. CMS develops a fee schedule for physicians, ambulance services, clinical laboratory services and durable medical equipment, prosthetics, orthotics, and supplies.

### 2.2.1.4    Trends in Payments

The reimbursement system has not always provided proper incentives to healthcare providers to employ their best practices. For example, the reimbursement system may not always pay for new treatments, even if they clearly are an improvement over the existing standard of care. Further, the

---

[13]   42 C.F.R. §§ 409.30–.35; U.S. Department of Health & Human Services, Centers for Medicare & Medicaid Services, *Medicare Intermediary Manual*, Part 3 § 3132, http://www.cms.hhs.gov/manuals/pbm/ItemDetail.asp?ItemID=CMS021918 (last visited April 30, 2008).

[14]   *See supra* note 12.

[15]   Social Security Act § 1813(a)(3); 42 U.S.C. § 1395e; 42 C.F.R. § 409.85.

[16]   U.S. Department of Health & Human Services, Centers for Medicare & Medicaid Services, *Medicare Intermediary Manual*, Part 3 §§ 3110, 3137, http://www.cms.hhs.gov/manuals/pbm/ItemDetail.asp?ItemID=CMS021918 (last visited Apr. 30, 2008).

[17]   Report to Congress: Medicare Payment Policy, MEDPAC, Mar. 2008, at 145, http://www.medpac.gov/chapters/Mar08_Ch02d.pdf (last visited Apr. 29, 2008).

traditional indemnity reimbursement system does not reward healthcare providers for providing a higher quality of care.

Within the past several years, however, CMS has implemented some demonstration pay-for-performance programs through the CMS Value-Based Purchasing initiative.[18] This program was authorized by the Medicare Prescription Drug Improvement and Modernization Act of 2003 and Deficit Reduction Act of 2005. Similarly, physicians can earn up to 1.5% of Medicare payments by participation in the Physician Quality Reporting Initiative. While this program is more "pay for reporting," CMS is expected to transition this program into a true pay-for-performance system similar to programs implemented by some private payors.

Currently, more than half of all states have implemented Medicaid pay for performance programs, with nearly 85% of states expected to have a pay-for-performance program within the next five years.[19]

Finally, CMS issued a new rule change whereby it will no longer pay for a provider's errors or services resulting in injuries. The intent of these programs is that they better align the interests of the healthcare providers with the interests of their consumers.

### 2.2.2    Managed Care

As healthcare costs began to rise in the 1970s and 1980s, payors developed mechanisms intended to control the costs of the provision of healthcare services. This paved the way for health insurance products such as HMOs and preferred provider organizations (PPOs). HMOs are similar to indemnity insurance companies in that HMOs are financially responsible for the entire cost of providing covered healthcare services to organizations insureds. HMOs charge a flat premium and are responsible for the delivery of healthcare services to enrollees on a prepaid basis, rather than an indemnity basis. HMOs can offer affordable healthcare services due to their use of certain managed care mechanisms discussed further below. Conversely, a PPO is an arrangement designed to provide incentives for enrollees to use certain designated healthcare providers who then supply services at a discounted rate. Self-insured companies often engage third party administrators to administer their self-insured plans using managed-care concepts.

One of the tenets of the first generation of managed care techniques was that the insurers covered only "medically necessary" services. Only later did insurers incorporate preventive medicine concepts in their managed care techniques, recognizing that by spending more upfront on preventive measures, insurers ultimately spend less. Another tenet of managed care is that patients are provided with incentives to use medical services in a cost-appropriate manner. For instance, patients are offered incentives to seek care in the most appropriate settings, and patients may incur a higher copayment or may not

---

[18] U.S. Department of Health & Human Services, Centers for Medicare & Medicaid Services, *Hospital Quality Initiatives–Overview,* http://www.cms.hhs.gov/HospitalQualityInits/ (last visited May 2, 2008). (For example, 250 hospitals are participating in a three-year Premier Hospital Quality Improvement Demonstration project.).

[19] K. Kuhmerker and T. Hartman, *Pay-for-Performance in State Medicaid Programs: A Survey of State Medicaid Directors and Programs*, The Commonwealth Fund, (Apr. 2007), *available at* http://www.commonwealthfund.org/publications/publications_show.htm?doc_id=472891.

be covered by seeking non-emergent care in a hospital emergency room as opposed to an outpatient clinic. With respect to the healthcare providers, HMOs also employ medical management techniques such as practice protocols, pre-authorization of certain services, utilization review, and quality assurance. Managed care organizations are also implementing tiered physician networks whereby patients are offered a financial incentive to obtain healthcare services from providers in the high tier.

HMOs also sought to control costs by utilizing primary care physicians as "gatekeepers" and sharing the insurance risk with healthcare providers. In a gatekeeper system, patients are required to see a primary care physician before being authorized to see specialist physicians, who tend to use more expensive procedures. Accordingly, if a patient has a rash, the patient first must see the primary care physician. Then, either the primary care physician will treat the patient or, if necessary, the physician will give the patient a referral to see a dermatologist. This way, HMOs are able to direct patients to seek out less expensive medical care prior to turning to more expensive medical procedures.

In addition, just as HMOs were financially responsible for the cost of providing healthcare services, HMOs began to make healthcare providers responsible for their cost of providing healthcare services. HMOs did this by restructuring the payment arrangements to physicians, hospitals and other healthcare providers. With physicians, and especially primary care physicians, HMOs would often pay physicians based upon a capitation methodology, *i.e.*, payments are determined on a per-patient, per-month basis. For example, the HMO could agree with a primary care physician that it will assign a certain number of the HMO's patients to that physician and that it will pay $100 per patient per month. If, in any given month, all of the HMO's patients are healthy, then the primary care physician takes home $100 per assigned patient without having to provide any services. If, however, a flu epidemic breaks out and a large percentage of the assigned patients become ill, then the physician is still paid $100 per patient per month, but is nonetheless required to provide all medically necessary services to those patients.

While many PPOs and HMOs pay hospitals on a discounted fee-for-service basis or on a discounted fixed rate per day of care, some HMOs employ similar capitation or "flat fee" methodologies for hospitals and other types of healthcare providers. With hospitals, HMOs may employ either per-diem reimbursement (a hospital is paid a flat amount for each day an HMO's patient is hospitalized, regardless of the reason such patient is hospitalized) or on a diagnostic related methodology (the hospital is paid a flat amount based upon the reason the patient is hospitalized). If an HMO is using a diagnostic related methodology and a patient has viral pneumonia, then the hospital is paid the flat amount that the HMO has set for that illness. As a result, whether the patient recovers quickly or if the patient recovers slowly, the hospital is paid the same flat fee. These cost-sharing reimbursement methods are intended to reward the healthcare provider for greater efficiency, but they also provide an incentive for healthcare providers to utilize less expensive services and products.

States have enacted various laws regulating the managed care industry. For example, a number of states have enacted laws mandating a minimum of 48-hour hospital stays for women after delivery, laws prohibiting "gag clauses" (contract provisions that prohibit providers from discussing various issues with their patients), laws defining "emergencies" which provide that a healthcare plan may not deny coverage for an emergency room visit if a layperson would perceive the situation as an emergency, and laws requiring direct access to obstetrician/gynecologists without the requirement of a referral from a primary-care physician.

Health plans, Medicare, Medicaid, employers, trade groups and other purchasers of health services, private standard-setting organizations, and accrediting agencies increasingly are using statistical and other measures in efforts to characterize, publicize, compare, rank, and change the quality, safety, and cost of healthcare services provided by hospitals and physicians. Published rankings, such as "score cards," pay-for-performance, and other financial and non-financial incentive programs are being introduced to assist consumers with selecting healthcare providers. This increased transparency affects the reputation and revenue of healthcare providers and influences the behavior of consumers and providers. Currently prevalent are measures of quality based on clinical outcomes of patient care, reduction in costs, patient satisfaction, and investment in health information technology.

### 2.2.3 Tort Law: What It Is, Why It's So Important in America, and How It Affects the Healthcare System

Tort law can be thought of as a middle ground between contract law and criminal law. Contract law creates private rights between A and B that arise from private agreements made by A and B. Criminal law also creates obligations (*e.g.*, A cannot assault B) imposed by society because society is also damaged every time A commits a crime against B. Crime, in this context, can be thought of as a *public* wrong-doing. Tort law is a hybrid of sorts between the private world of contract and the public world of criminal wrong-doing. Tort liability does not generally arise from any private agreement between A and B, nor does a tort usually involve criminal behavior that affects society at large, although overlaps do exist. Anglo-Saxon jurisprudence construes a tort as a *private* wrong inflicted on a person by another person, for which the victim may be "made whole." Accordingly, the tort system contemplates that the victim must be compensated in a manner so that the victim is returned, to the greatest extent possible, to his status or condition prior to the commission of the tort.

The rights of the individual and the notions of private rights and private wrongs are at the very center of the American system of jurisprudence. Accordingly, tort law is viewed by many as serving a valuable administrative and enforcement function.

Tort law in the United States affects the delivery of healthcare services in multiple ways. As discussed above, medical malpractice lawsuits can have the effect of causing healthcare providers to practice defensive medicine, thereby increasing the cost of the delivery of healthcare. Similarly, due to increased transparency, consumers of healthcare services have access to information regarding malpractice awards. Consequently, payors and patients may be disinclined to utilize the services of a provider with high or multiple awards. The high cost of malpractice insurance has caused some healthcare providers to move to other areas (causing a shortage of availability of certain specialists, such as obstetricians), to "self insure," or to create captive offshore insurance trusts.

### 2.2.4    Fraud and Abuse Issues

Federal and state healthcare fraud and abuse laws regulate both the provision of services to government program beneficiaries and the methods and requirements for submitting claims for services rendered to such beneficiaries. Fraud and abuse cases may be prosecuted by one or more government entities and/or private individuals, and more than one of the available penalties may be imposed for each violation. Federal and state governments have a range of criminal, civil, and administrative sanctions available to penalize and remediate healthcare fraud and abuse, including exclusion of the provider from participation in the Medicare/Medicaid programs, fines, civil monetary penalties, and suspension of payments and, in the case of individuals, imprisonment. Under these laws, individuals and organizations can be penalized for submitting claims for services that were not provided, billed in a manner other than as actually provided, not medically necessary, provided by an improper person, accompanied by an illegal inducement to utilize or refrain from utilizing a service or product, or billed in a manner that does not otherwise comply with applicable government requirements.

Laws governing fraud and abuse apply to all individuals and healthcare enterprises with which a healthcare provider does business including hospitals, home health agencies, long-term care entities, infusion providers, pharmaceutical providers, insurers, HMOs, PPOs, third party administrators, physicians, physician groups, and service companies.

The federal government has expended vast resources to combat fraud and abuse in the healthcare industry and has recovered billions of dollars in improperly billed healthcare services. Moreover, the federal government provides incentives for whistle blowers to report healthcare providers or entities that engage in false billing by permitting the whistle blower to share in the recovered amount. Congress has sought to limit fraud and conflicts of interest in the healthcare industry by enacting the Anti-Kickback Statute,[20] the Stark Amendment,[21] and the False Claims Act,[22] each of which will be discussed below.

### 2.2.4.1    *The Anti-Kickback Statute*

The Anti-Kickback Statute provides that it is unlawful to knowingly and willfully offer, pay, solicit, or receive any remuneration for the referral of items or services for which payment may be made by the Medicare or Medicaid programs. Violation of the Anti-Kickback Statute is a felony, subject to significant civil and criminal penalties, as well as exclusion from the Medicare and Medicaid programs.

Since the Anti-Kickback Statute's prohibitions are very broad, the Office of the Inspector General of the Department of Health and Human Services (OIG) has promulgated certain "safe harbors"

---

[20]   42 U.S.C. § 1320a-7b(6).
[21]   42 U.S.C. § 1395nn.
[22]   31 U.S.C. § 3729. *See also* Taxpayers Against Fraud Education Fund, State False Claims Acts, http://www.taf.org/statefca.htm (last visited May 2, 2008). (Most states have enacted their own state versions of these laws, thereon extending the prohibition from relating to Medicare and Medicaid items and services to the delivery of all healthcare items and services.)

protecting certain activities and relationships from being deemed to violate the Anti-Kickback Statute. The following are examples of activities covered by the safe harbors:

- investment interests in public companies;

- space and equipment rentals, provided that written agreements are entered into for at least one year and the compensation is set in advance and not based on the volume or value of referrals generated between the parties;

- personal services and management contracts, provided that written agreements are entered into for at least one year and the compensation is set in advance and not based on the volume or value of referrals generated between the parties;

- sale of a physician practice, provided that the sale is not to a hospital and the selling physician may not refer patients for one year;

- employment agreements, provided that written agreements are entered into for at least one year, and the compensation is set in advance and not based on the volume or value of referrals generated between the parties; and

- other investment interests, provided that any investor in a position to refer or generate referrals for the entity may not own, control or receive any remuneration from the entity in excess of 40% of the interests in the aggregate.

From time to time, the OIG issues Fraud Alerts in an effort to raise its concerns about various healthcare industry practices. For example, in prior Fraud Alerts, the OIG has targeted hospital incentives provided to physicians that are intended to boost referrals, such as discounted office space or nursing staff, payment for administrative services provided by physicians to hospitals, interest-free loans, and income guarantees. The OIG also has sought to limit certain of the pharmaceutical industry's marketing and sales practices. For example, the OIG has scrutinized gifts to physicians, use of physicians as consults, and awarding grants to physicians that require very little work on the part of the physician.

To help administer the Anti-Kickback Statute, the OIG opines, through its advisory opinion process, on whether an activity in question would fall within the scope of the Anti-Kickback Statute. These opinions often are useful in determining whether analogous activities would incur potential liability under the Anti-Kickback Statute. Similarly, the OIG has issued form compliance plans for various types of healthcare providers. The adoption and compliance with these compliance plans can limit a healthcare provider's potential liability under the Anti-Kickback Statute.

### 2.2.4.2  The Stark Amendment

The Stark Amendment prohibits a physician from making a referral for any "designated health services" payable under the Medicare or Medicaid programs to any entity in which the physician has an ownership or compensation arrangement. Unlike the Anti-Kickback Statute, the Stark Amendment provides for a *per se* violation and no proof of intent is required for a violation to occur. The Stark Amendment also provides that any party found to have violated its provisions may be subject to civil penalties and exclusion from Medicare.

The "Designated Health Services" subject to the Stark Amendment are as follows:

- clinical laboratory services;
- physical therapy services;
- occupational therapy services;
- radiology services;
- radiation therapy services;
- durable medical equipment;
- parenteral and enteral nutrients, equipment and supplies;
- home health services;
- outpatient prescription drugs; and
- inpatient and outpatient hospital services.

The Stark Amendment does, however, provide for certain exceptions to its restrictions. Subject to various restrictions, the exceptions include referrals for Designated Health Services within a physician's own group practice, leases of office space, and employment agreements. Similar to the Anti-Kickback Statute, CMS will provide an advisory opinion as to whether or not a certain arrangement or practice falls within the scope of the Stark Amendment. However, the advisory opinion process has been considerably less robust than the advisory opinion process under the Anti-Kickback Statute.

### 2.2.4.3   The False Claims Act

The False Claims Act imposes civil liability on a person or corporation for, among other things:

- knowingly presenting or cause to be presented a false or fraudulent claim for payment to the United States;
- knowingly using a false record or statement to obtain payment on a false or fraudulent claim paid by the United States; or
- engaging in a conspiracy to defraud the United States to obtain allowance for or payment of a false or fraudulent claim.

The False Claims Act defines "knowingly" as having actual knowledge of the falsity of the claim, acting in deliberate ignorance of the truth or the falsity of the claim, or acting in reckless disregard of the truth or falsity of the claim. No proof of specific intent to defraud is required.

To aid in the enforcement of the False Claims Act, the act permits private individuals, known as *qui tam* plaintiffs or relators, to institute actions against any person or corporation. If the government decides not to intervene in any *qui tam* action, the *qui tam* plaintiff may pursue the False Claims Act action on his or her own. To encourage private individuals to institute an action for violations of the False Claims Act, the False Claims Act permits a *qui tam* plaintiff to receive a percentage of the government's recovery (typically 25% to 30% if government does not intervene; 15 to 25% if the government does intervene). In addition, since *qui tam* plaintiffs often are current or former employees of the defendant, the False Claims Act specifically protects any person instituting a *qui tam* action against a retaliatory discharge or demotion.

A civil action under the False Claims Act brought by a *qui tam* plaintiff must be commenced no later than: (1) six years after the date on which the False Claims Act violation is committed, or (2) three years after the date when facts material to the right of action are known or reasonably should have been known by the *qui tam* plaintiff, whichever occurs last. A suit under the False Claims Act must, in any event, be brought no more than 10 years after the date on which the violation occurred.

### 2.2.5    Antitrust

The other noteworthy area of federal oversight is in the area of antitrust enforcement. The federal government has enacted antitrust restrictions that prohibit monopolies and monopolistic behavior as well as anti-competitive behavior, such as price fixing. For example, the federal government has blocked certain healthcare mergers on the theory that such mergers would result in diminished competition and thus lead to higher prices. Similarly, the federal government has prosecuted networks of physicians from collectively negotiating with healthcare insurers on the theory that such activities are anti-competitive. The FTC and the DOJ have issued joint policy statements addressed to the healthcare industry governing specific aspects of healthcare industry. For example, the FTC and DOJ will not challenge certain types of hospital mergers if such mergers fall within certain designated criteria.

### 2.2.6    Licensing

Virtually every healthcare provider, including hospitals, physicians, and healthcare practitioners, must be licensed in order to operate. Generally, this licensure takes place at the state level. Many states also have "corporate practice of medicine" laws which prohibit licensed medical providers from being employed by and practicing medicine through corporate entities, except for professional corporations or hospitals. At the institutional level, hospitals, clinics, ambulatory surgical centers, and nursing homes all require governmental licenses in order to operate. Health insurers such as HMOs, PPOs, and traditional indemnity insurers are licensed and regulated by a state's department of insurance. In some states, HMOs are treated more like healthcare providers than insurance companies and, thus, are regulated by a state's department of health rather than the department of insurance. Similarly, some states regulate continuing care retirement communities as an insurance product as opposed to a health facility.

#### 2.2.6.1    *Certificates of Need*

Certain types of healthcare entities such as hospitals, surgical centers, and nursing homes must undergo additional regulatory requirements in certain states. During the 1970s, healthcare costs rose dramatically. In response to rising healthcare costs in the 1970s, many states enacted certificate of need (CON) laws that require healthcare providers to justify certain expenditures prior to their existence. CON laws will also govern any change of ownership of a facility. Some states allow for an expedited review and approval process for certain changes pursuant to a certificate of exemption. Some states will allow a healthcare facility to relocate certified beds to other locations and changes in the approved use of such certified beds, creating the ability of a healthcare entity to have swing beds to be used for different purposes or locations.

Many states, however, have begun to let market forces determine whether certain medical expenditures should be made instead of a state regulatory agency. Many states, including Minnesota, Pennsylvania and California, have abolished their CON laws entirely. Other states, such as Georgia, Wisconsin and Ohio, have relaxed their CON requirements. For example, legislation is pending in Florida that would eliminate CON requirements for the establishment of hospitals.[23] The Federal Trade Commission has submitted testimony to the Florida Senate supporting the elimination of certain CON requirements as a means to encourage competition.[24]

### 2.2.6.2  *Ramifications of Extensive Licensing for Equity Financings*

The sale of a healthcare business can be effected through sale of all of the business's assets or through the sale of the owners' equity interests in the business. A sale of all of the assets may have significant benefits to a buyer (including the limitation of liabilities), but would require the re-licensing of the purchaser in most instances. Many types of licenses, healthcare licenses especially, cannot be transferred from seller to buyer, and the buyer is forced to reapply for licenses in its own name and based on its own qualifications in order to use a seller's assets. The process can be slow, cumbersome, and uncertain. Accordingly, buyers often purchase the equity interests in the business, thereby stepping into the shoes of former equity holders, requiring no change in licensure to operate the assets. However, stock sales normally require a buyer to assume all of the target's liabilities. Further, many regulatory agencies require notification and approval for any change in control of a licensed healthcare entity. Even where equity is simply being purchased but no buy-out is intended or majority interest conveyed, licensing authorities may rescind the license based on a perceived "change in control" in the licensee caused by a significant change in identity of insiders and "controlling" shareholders.

## 2.3  **Payment Issues**

The manner in which the healthcare industry makes its money has much in common with the legal industry, both of which are service industries that generally produce no tangible product. In each industry, services are exchanged for cash, or more likely for what is supposed to be a short term IOU— the receivable. Once services are provided, they cannot be taken back if the receivable is never paid or if a customer refuses to pay the entire debt. However, in the healthcare industry, the actual payor of the service is often a different party than the consumer of the service.

Thus, it is crucial to any so-called cash-and-carry industry to parlay as great a percentage of total receivables generated into collected cash. Cash, in turn, is the most important asset. In order to increase revenue, a healthcare provider must charge more for services, collect on a higher percentage

---

[23]  2008 Fla. S.B. 2326.
[24]  Federal Trade Commission and the Department of Justice, "Improving Health Care: A Dose of Competition," 22, (July 2004), http://www.justice.gov/atr/public/health_care/204694.pdf. (In July 2004, the Federal Trade Commission and the Department of Justice jointly served a report entitled "Improving Health Care: A Dose of Competition," in which the agencies indicated that CON programs "are not successful in containing health care costs, and that they pose serious anti-competitive risks that usually outweigh their purported economic benefits.").

of receivables generated, or increase "throughput" in the system by providing even more services. In the healthcare industry, payors often set the price paid for services, providers have historically struggled in collection efforts, and increased throughput often requires increased capital.

As discussed above, the healthcare industry's dependence on powerful third party payors for a significant portion of its cash flow creates special collection problems. Unpredictable payor behavior leaves the industry financially vulnerable and makes the private financing of healthcare more difficult and expensive.

### 2.3.1    Special Legal Characteristics of Governmental Receivables

#### 2.3.1.1    *The Uniform Commercial Code*

Revised Article 9 of the Uniform Commercial Code (the UCC) includes healthcare insurance receivables as a subset of Accounts.[25] Under the UCC, a healthcare provider can grant a lender a security interest in healthcare insurance receivables, and the lender can then perfect such security interest by filing a financing statement under UCC § 9-310. However a prudent lender will also enter into deposit account control agreements with the banks and other financial institutions that receive the cash generated by such Accounts. Otherwise, a competing lender's "control" of the relevant deposit accounts will trump a security interest in Accounts perfected through a mere filing.[26] Control agreements will also subordinate the host banks' superior right of recourse to the proceeds of the Accounts which they would otherwise enjoy under UCC § 9-327(3). While these UCC concepts apply generally to both government paid and private payor receivables, government receivables offer a second layer of complexity because of certain applicable anti-assignment laws, discussed below.

#### 2.3.1.2    *Anti-Assignment Laws*

Federal law prohibits Medicare or Medicaid accounts receivable to be held in an account controlled by a third party other than the Medicare or Medicaid participating provider.[27] Prior to the creation of the Medicare anti-assignment laws, healthcare providers were selling or "factoring" their rights to receive payment from the federal government to third parties in exchange for immediate cash at a discount on face value of the receivable. These third party factors then sought collection on the receivables from the federal government. There were substantial concerns about the third party factors submitting overstated claims and confusion regarding the identities of the healthcare service providers and claimants.

To cure these ills, Congress passed laws preventing healthcare providers from selling or "assigning" their receivables to others or allowing any party other than the provider to receive direct payment from the government.[28] The unintended consequence of these laws, unfortunately, has been confusion and uncertainty for healthcare lenders and providers.

---

[25]  U.C.C. § 9-102(2) (2001).
[26]  U.C.C. § 9-327 (2001).
[27]  42 U.S.C. §§ 1395b(c), 1395b-6; 42 C.F.R. §§ 424.71–.80.
[28]  42 U.S.C. § 1395g(c); 42 C.F.R. § 424.80.

It is not possible to enter into a typical secured lending arrangement in which the borrower grants the lender the right to stand in borrower's shoes and collect payments directly from the government. This form of collateral is, in other lending contexts, a very useful, effective, and simple device. This is especially true in cash-and-carry industries where payment rights are the primary asset that the borrower hypothecates.

Transactional lawyers devise ways to overcome the anti-assignment laws. One involves a "double-lock box" device in which payments from the government are made first to an account controlled by the healthcare provider. Amounts are then automatically and routinely swept out of that account into another account controlled by the lender. Because payments are first made to an account controlled by the healthcare provider, the government is not making payments to a third party. The government insists that the provider have the ability to stop amounts from being automatically swept into the second account. This legal structure allows the borrower to be more than a mere conduit for payments made directly between the government and the lender. Lenders can then obtain contractual assurances and protections to discourage the borrower from actually exercising its right to cease the routine sweeps of the deposit account. Lenders, nevertheless, must take on the extra risk that a provider would nonetheless stop the sweeps.

### 2.3.1.3   The True-Up process

Even when the government remits payment to a healthcare provider, lenders still cannot be certain that the government will not take back the money later on. This has disastrous results for both borrower and lender.

Under the current system, Medicare payments are made to providers throughout the year for services provided before such claims can be audited and verified. At the end of the year, an itemized cost report is submitted by the provider, and the payment agents working on behalf of the government determine whether the provider underpaid or overpaid. If the government has overpaid, it has a number of methods for addressing the overpayment, including set-offs against future payments, property seizures, and withdrawing provider eligibility. Thus, at the end of every year, many healthcare providers paid by Medicare roll the dice, to some degree, not knowing for certain how the true-up process will treat them that year. Lenders are used to being in control rather than helpless in the face of bureaucratic vicissitudes; for them the helpless feeling caused by the true-up process is too often an invitation to exit the healthcare finance industry.

### 2.3.1.4   Borrower Vulnerability to Set-Off and Other Enforcement Actions

If the true-up process reveals overpayment, the government may set-off or recoup against receivables in the current period until the overpayments are recouped. Indeed, the government can assert a right to set-off against healthcare receivables not only for overpayments related to healthcare, but for practically any other debt the government perceives it is owed by the provider. Consequently, a lender needs to concern itself with whether receivables for the current reimbursement period may be set-off because of the borrower's tax, ERISA, or social securities liabilities.

Bankruptcy has the general effect of wiping out past debts and giving incoming lenders a clean slate to lend against (assuming positive cash flow from operations). However, even bankruptcy may provide no protection from the government's recoupment rights. A pre-bankruptcy debt owed to the government may be recouped from amounts owing to a provider by the government, even where such amounts arise from services rendered *after* the bankruptcy petition was filed.[29]

### 2.3.1.5    Privacy Issues

With healthcare receivables collateral, lenders and healthcare providers need to be aware of confidentiality issues relating to receivables. A lender's customary due diligence on such receivables, as well as monitoring and realizing on collateral, may expose the lender to protected health information. Both state and federal law restrict a healthcare provider's use and disclosure of a patient's protected health information.[30] A healthcare provider's general consent form may be sufficiently broad to permit disclosures related to the healthcare provider's general business purposes. Similarly, the Health Insurance Portability and Accountability Act of 1996 (HIPAA) allows a healthcare provider to disclose protected health information for "healthcare operations." Healthcare operations include quality assurance, credentialing and general administrative activities.[31] Financing receivables likely falls within this definition. Healthcare providers may disclose protected health information to a "business associate" so long as a business associate agreement is in place. Accordingly, healthcare providers may require a lender to sign a business associate agreement[32] as a result of any disclosures related to receivables. Alternatively, lenders may request information in an encoded fashion, to avoid any disclosures of protected health information.

### 2.3.2    Private Third Party Payors

The vast majority of medical bills and invoices generated in the United States are not paid by the patient, but rather by insurance companies, HMOs and other private payor organizations. Such payors often enter into contractual pre-arrangements with the healthcare providers as to how much such providers may charge for particular services and procedures. Persons receiving coverage from private payors often do so on the condition that they only receive services from payor-approved healthcare providers (or else pay themselves for out-of-plan services). Not surprisingly, payors bring real economic power to bear in their dealings with healthcare providers. Providers who do not meet payor demands may find that hundreds of potential patients covered by such payors may not be able to do business with such providers. Private payors are also privately funded, most commonly through payments received from the patients' employers. Private payors are often adequately capitalized, sophisticated, and capable of dealing with healthcare service providers from a position of strength. These characteristics mean that third party payors may pay fairly well, given the total size of a particular bill or invoice, but will often still insist on significant discounts. Some third party payors are also notoriously slow in paying their debts to providers in order to benefit from the "float" time of maintaining possession of such funds until the last possible moment. In response, states have increasingly enacted prompt pay laws to require payors to pay healthcare providers within prescribed time periods.

---

[29]   *See, e.g., In re CDM Management Services, Inc.*, 226 B.R. 195 (Bankr., S.D. Ind. 1997).
[30]   45 C.F.R. § 164.
[31]   45 C.F.R. § 164.501.
[32]   45 C.F.R. § 164.508.

### 2.3.3    The Resulting Importance of Payor Mix

In a cash-and-carry industry, the source of a borrower's cash flow is crucial. Understanding a borrower's so-called payor mix and the habits and proclivities of each type of payor is crucial to any lender. Medicare tends to pay its bills at a steady rate but with significant discounts to the amounts charged and subject to annual true-up. Medicaid varies state by state, as it is a hybrid federal-state program, but generally pays less than Medicare and can be erratic. That said, Medicaid can pay quickly when funds are available. A small healthcare business with greater dependency on Medicaid receivables may have chronic cash flow problems. Private insurance payors tend to pay higher amounts per claim than public payors but also tend to be slow payors. Patients who directly pay for services pay the highest and the quickest. However, healthcare providers are often least-equipped to collect money from private individuals. Similarly, consumer groups have been very active in publicizing and litigating disparities in the amounts charged to private individuals as compared to the discounted amounts negotiated with managed care or governmental payors. Payment under managed care programs, such as HMOs and PPOs, vary greatly depending on the quality and scope of services under the various plans.

Savvy lenders will generally know a borrower's payor mix and be aware of general reimbursement trends for each type of payor. Loan documents and risk premiums can then be adjusted based on this knowledge. Lenders often also study the types of services offered to assess coverage from the preferred classes of third party payors. For example, nursing homes that can offer certain types of services, such as physical therapy, are more likely to be eligible for Medicare payments. Usually, the erosion of a desirable payor mix is often a sign of difficult future financial performance.

# 3

# Types of Potential Healthcare Providers Needing Capital

As described thus far, healthcare is a highly capital intensive service industry. However, the need for external capital varies across the industry by provider type. This **Chapter 3** describes the major healthcare provider categories and the capital demands of each.

## 3.1 Hospitals

Hospitals no longer dominate America's healthcare system as they once did.[1] Now they share the market with a wide variety of competing healthcare providers. Some of these competing providers may even call themselves hospitals but do not have emergency rooms and other ancillary services customarily associated with a hospital. Such specialty hospitals focus on the care of a particular body part or physiological system, such as heart hospitals, in an attempt to maximize efficiency, expertise, and profitability.[2]

Even with hospitals now having to share market space, they still are the single most important type of healthcare provider. In 2006, hospitals consumed nearly 31% of all U.S. healthcare expenditures, and, in combination with traditional physician and clinical services, about 52% of the total budget.[3] So recent changes and trends notwithstanding (*see* **Chapter 1**), the old players still dominate healthcare.

### 3.1.1 Not-for-Profit Hospitals

Not-for-profit hospitals constitute at least 60% of the more than 3,400 U.S. hospitals.[4] The not-for-profit description can easily mislead the uninitiated; it does not prevent hospitals from selling medical goods and services to the public at a profit. Rather, what separates not-for-profit from for-profit enterprises is that not-for-profit entities are not permitted to distribute profits to shareholders. The profits must be reinvested in the corporation. Consequently, some not-for-profits have, perhaps counter-intuitively, a great deal of cash on their balance sheets. Recent data collected by the *Wall Street Journal*

---

[1] According to data from the American Hospital Association, the number of hospital beds in the U.S. fell from just over 1 million in 1982 to 808,000 in 2004, while the number of beds per 1,000 population declined from 4.37 to 2.75, indicating that consumers are increasingly accessing healthcare services in outpatient settings such as medical office buildings and freestanding or outpatient clinics.

[2] David Whelan, *Stop that Patient*, Forbes, Mar 10, 2008, at 90.

[3] Matthew Dobias, *Shock to the System*, Modern Healthcare Magazine, Jan. 14, 2008.

[4] John Carreyrou and Barbara Martinez, *Nonprofit Hospitals, Once for the Poor, Strike It Rich*, Wall Street Journal, Apr. 4, 2008, at A1.

indicates that at least 25 not-for-profit hospitals or hospital systems earn more than $250 million annually.[5] Indeed, critics of not-for-profit hospitals allege that they are taking advantage of their tax benefits and their relatively low cost of capital without conferring on society the so-called charity care that the tax breaks were supposed to inspire. In recent years, healthcare providers have faced increasing challenges regarding whether their operations and practices are consistent with the regulatory requirements for non-profit tax-exempt organizations. Non-profit hospitals are experiencing increased scrutiny in areas such as pricing practices, billing and collection practices, charitable care, executive compensation, exemption of property from real property taxation, and others. These challenges have come from a variety of sources, including state attorneys general, the Internal Revenue Service, labor unions, Congress, state legislatures, and patients, and in a variety of forums, including hearings, audits, and litigation.

Since 2004, three Congressional Committees have conducted hearings and other proceedings inquiring into various practices of non-profit hospitals and health agencies. The House Committee on Energy and Commerce launched a nationwide investigation of hospital billing and collection practices and prices charged to uninsured patients. The House Committee requested 20 large hospital and healthcare systems to provide detailed historical charge and billing practice information for acute care services. The House Committee on Ways and Means has also held several hearings to examine the tax-exempt sector and hospital tax-exemption and the use of tax-preferred bond financing.

The Senate Finance Committee also conducted hearings on required reforms to the non-profit sector and released a staff discussion draft on proposals for reform in the area of tax-exempt organizations, including a proposal for a five-year review of tax-exempt status by the Internal Revenue Service (IRS). The Senate Committee also requested information from a number of non-profit hospitals and hospital systems regarding their charitable activities, patient billing, and ventures with for-profit corporations and hospitals.

In August 2004, the IRS announced a new enforcement effort to identify and halt abuses by tax-exempt organizations that pay excessive compensation and benefits to their officers and other insiders. The IRS announced that it would contact nearly 2,000 charities and foundations to seek more information about their compensation practices and procedures. The IRS began its enforcement project at the end of July 2004 and it has continued into 2008.

It is estimated that 77% of not-for-profits operate profitably, whereas only 61% of for-profit hospitals are profitable.[6] In response, some state taxing authorities have sought to reverse some of the tax benefits conferred on non-profit hospitals due to the hospitals' failure to provide sufficient charity care. In Illinois, for example, the Illinois Department of Revenue sought to deny Provena Covenant Medical Center's charitable and religions property tax exemption.[7]

Not-for-profit healthcare providers are also targeted in lawsuits in federal and state courts across the country regarding billing and collection practices relating to the uninsured. The lawsuits are pre-

---

[5] *Id.*

[6] *Id.*

[7] *See* Medical News Today.com, *High Earnings at Some Not-for-Profit Hospitals Draws Criticism of Tax-Exempt Status*, available at http://www.medicalnewstoday.com/articles/102951.php.

mised on the notion that federal and state laws require non-profit healthcare providers to provide certain levels of free or discounted healthcare to the uninsured. Plaintiffs allege, among other things, that the defendant violated federal and state law by billing the uninsured at undiscounted rates, that the medical bills sent to the uninsured are inflated, and that the defendants engaged in unfair debt collection practices.

In 2009, new standards will go into effect that require not-for-profits to publicly disclose the amount of the charity care that they provide.[8] Still, no law has been proposed that would set forth a minimum level of charity care that must be provided to qualify as a not-for-profit hospital.

### 3.1.2    For-Profit Hospitals

For-profit hospitals function much the same as other corporations, with shareholders (or members), a board of directors, and various officers. For-profit hospitals also function similarly to non-profit hospitals in that there is a separate medical staff and medical staff by-laws.

For-profit hospitals must attract patients in open competition with other types of healthcare providers and with other hospitals. Hospitals seek to maximize services that are highly profitable (*e.g.*, heart surgery) while de-emphasizing practice areas that are not easily lucrative without intensive specialization and investment (*e.g.*, mental health services). For-profit hospitals must go where the demand is, but all things being equal, many would also prefer to go where the money is, meaning a preference for a wealthier patient population. For-profit hospitals worry about their public image and the prestige and image of their brand. For-profit hospitals, like other cash-and-carry service providers, must also control their costs and their risks.

Hospital profitability can be highly cyclical. Investment in new infrastructure must be made to remain competitive and to attract physicians and patients. These investments then reap rewards for a number of years. By then, new technologies, equipment, and procedures are available and a new round of investment is required to obtain them. Many for-profit hospitals have looked to physicians as a source of capital. Physician investment and ownership in hospitals creates an alignment of interests. However, the OIG has expressed concerns from a fraud and abuse perspective, since physician ownership of hospitals creates an incentive and inducement for referrals and over-utilization. Accordingly, physician ownership of hospitals and other healthcare facilities must be closely scrutinized for compliance with the Anti-Kickback Statute and the Stark Amendment.[9]

## 3.2    Long Term Care Facilities

### 3.2.1    Types

The following is a description of the common types of long term care facilities, as well as their common acronyms:

---

[8]  Dobias, *Shock to the System*, at A1.
[9]  Carreyrou and Martinez, *Nonprofit Hospitals, Once for the Poor, Strike It Rich*, at A1.

### 3.2.1.1   Independent Living Facilities

Independent living facilities (ILFs) are generally multifamily rental properties targeted to seniors of a certain age. Congregate care is similar to independent living but features more of a community environment. ILFs, or congregate care facilities, offer other services and amenities such as meals, transportation, pools, a convenience store, bank, barber/beauty shop, housekeeping, laundry, and social and recreational activities, for a monthly fee. ILFs do not provide residents with assistance with activities of daily living or any healthcare services, such as supervision of medication, bathing, dressing, or home healthcare services. ILFs are generally not subject to any particular licensing requirements, and the services rendered by ILFs are not subject to reimbursement by any insurers or other healthcare payors.

### 3.2.1.2   Assisted Living Facilities

Assisted living facilities (ALFs) are state regulated facilities that provide the same services as ILFs, but also provide, in a majority of the units, supportive care to residents who require assistance with activities of daily living, such as medication management, bathing, dressing, ambulating, and eating. These facilities are designed to bridge the gap between independent living and nursing home care. Many ALFs have areas dedicated to residents with Alzheimer's or other forms of dementia. Like ILFs, residents generally pay a set monthly fee based upon the level of services rendered.

### 3.2.1.3   Skilled Nursing Facilities

Skilled nursing facilities (SNFs) are licensed healthcare facilities providing 24-hour nursing, rehabilitation and/or medical care. In many cases, SNFs are participating providers in the Medicaid and/or Medicare programs.

### 3.2.1.4   Continuing Care Retirement Communities

Continuing care retirement communities (CCRCs) are age-restricted properties that include a combination of independent living, assisted living, and skilled nursing services. These services are available to residents at a single facility or on a campus. The payments made by residents vary greatly. Some fees are based upon entrance fees, condominium or cooperative type programs, master trust arrangements, or simple rental amounts. Many CCRCs offer life care contracts, whereby residents pay a fee and the facility, in turn, assumes the responsibility to care for the resident's healthcare needs for the remainder of the resident's life. Most states regulate CCRCs as healthcare facilities. Some states instead regulate CCRCs as insurance products to the extent the CCRC offers life care contracts. Entrance of residents into CCRCs often correlates to the housing market. Potential residents often need to sell their existing homes to fund entrance fees. Accordingly, during a poor housing market, new entrants into CCRCs often decline. Similarly, residents in the independent living portions of CCRCs are sometimes reluctant to move into the assisted living portions of the CCRCs, instead electing to avail themselves of home health services. CCRCs seek to ensure that residents are residing in the appropriate part of the facility to reduce any potential liability regarding the care provided. Similarly, if a CCRC has a waiting list, the facility may be motivated to open space in the independent living facility.

### 3.2.2    The Present State of the Long Term Care Market

The lending market for long term care facilities has been marked with high-profile bankruptcies, over-saturation of markets, increased insurance costs, staffing shortages, and volatile reimbursement rates. Accordingly, while population and aging trends would indicate a more booming long term care market, some lenders and investors have not embraced the long term care industry.

Lending to long term care providers generally requires specialized underwriting, often involving market feasibility studies, demographic information, reimbursement rates, staffing ratios, and actuarial studies. To account for increased regulatory risk, lenders often require additional credit support from long term care facilities, such as additional collateral or guarantees as part of any loan facility. The long term care industry combines characteristics of real estate investment and service industry-based investment, relying on account receivables as well as property values for a significant portion of the collateral support. In addition, lending risks cannot be properly assessed without an understanding of the reimbursement aspects of the industry and regulatory requirements (as disclosed above). The increased prevalence of long term care insurance has improved the outlook for parts of the long term care industry. Traditionally, only services provided in skilled nursing facilities were subject to reimbursement. Long term care facilities also encounter many additional risks, such as environmental issues, ADA requirements, land use, and zoning. Long term care facilities are also highly regulated, often requiring certificates of need, extensive licensure, and Medicare and Medicaid participation. Despite the prevalence of national chains and REIT investments, generally the long term care market is thought of by consumers as a highly localized business, involving an understanding of the local market, demographics, culture, and community.

Long term care facilities have similar capital needs as hospitals. Aging facilities need capital improvements, and regulatory scrutiny also leads to required capital improvements. Often, skilled labor, operations, and technology are large cost components for long term care facilities.

### 3.2.3    Financial Evaluation of Long Term Care Facility Operations

#### 3.2.3.1    *Routine Indicators*

To some degree, the evaluation of a long term care facility will use many of the normal financial metrics used for other potential borrowers. In deciding to make a loan to a long term care facility, lenders usually evaluate, among other things, the amount of the requested loan to the overall value of the property, or collateral. Similarly, especially in acquisition financing, lenders often review the amount of the loan as a percentage of the overall cost of the transaction or value of collateral. These metrics include traditional earnings measuring devices such as EBITDA,[10] cash flow measurements, leverage ratios such as debt-to-EBITDA, overall net worth or "book value" of a business, and capitalization rates. Other special, healthcare-specific factors are reviewed, such as occupancy rates per total number of beds and vacancy factors.

---

[10]  EBITDA is an acronym standing for earnings before interest, taxes, depreciation, and amortization. EBITDA is a measurement of the earnings (*i.e.*, profits) a company *would have made* if it did not have to pay interest, taxes, and depreciation. EBITDA is useful because it allows an analyst to compare on a level playing field the performance of two companies with differing accounting and cash management policies. EBITDA is not, however, a measurement of operating cash flow. A company with a high EBITDA may have to shut its doors if it cannot convert its receivables and other paper profits into cash. EBIDA is used by non-profit companies, since taxes are not a factor.

### 3.2.3.2 Special Indicators

The qualitative analyses often make evaluation of long term care facilities special. These include a study of local culture to ascertain whether a particular hospital or nursing center happens to provides the types of services that are locally valued. Local markets may vary widely based on culture, demographics, and the relative wealth of the local population. The local payor mix might make a particular business model fail in certain communities and succeed a relatively short distance away. An evaluation of the personalities and skills of officers, directors and caregivers is especially important because potential customers (and their concerned families) will almost certainly be paying close attention to the same things.

## 3.3    Life Science Companies

Life science companies generally refer to pharmaceutical or biotechnology companies. A lender's collateral in a pharmaceutical company generally consists of patents, intellectual property, cash and accounts receivable. Accordingly, lenders closely monitor intellectual property and regulatory actions. A pharmaceutical company's cash flow needs are often influenced by patent protection for various drug products. For a branded pharmaceutical company, the loss of patent protection often leads to loss of revenue for that product. On the other hand, a loss of patent protection can lead to a significant opportunity for a generic company. Generic pharmaceutical companies also benefit from managed care initiatives. Pharmaceutical companies' performance can also be influenced by changes in reimbursement.

Pharmaceutical companies' working capital needs vary based upon research and development needs and the pharmaceutical industry can be capital intensive. Use of loan proceeds for pharmaceutical companies are generally for working capital purposes and for the funding of research and development. Funding is usually based upon a multiple of EBITDA or operating cash flow. Accordingly, life science companies are often subject to minimum EBITDA requirements. Some lenders are willing to issue debt to development stage, or pre-clinical stage, life science companies that are not cash flow positive, usually if such companies are sponsored by a strong venture or private equity fund. At any early stage, loans are generally structured as working capital loans secured by all assets of the life science company, with a lender relying on the company's intellectual property and strength of management and equity capital backing for security. Some lenders will also require the issuance of warrants in connection with a debt financing. Many life science companies are moving operations overseas. Both off-shoring of manufacturing and research and development are common. Accordingly, lenders must understand foreign-held collateral.

## 3.4    Medical Device and Equipment Manufacturers

Medical device manufacturers have more in common with pharmaceutical companies than with organizations treating patients. Their need for capital and the financial life-cycle of their products is also similar. Medical device manufacturers make heavy capital outlays to develop products that may never prove economically successful in practice. Perhaps only one product among many initially developed may actually prove profitable. Accordingly, medical device companies' most significant cash needs relate to research and development. Intellectual property law will often determine how long any one success story is able to corner the market before imitation devices lower margins. Smaller, more entrepreneurial companies face significant barriers to market entry given the high amount of capitalization necessary to bring a product successfully to market.

## 3.5    Other Healthcare Providers and Service Companies

### 3.5.1    Ambulatory Surgical Centers

Ambulatory Surgical Centers (ASCs) are often also known as outpatient surgery centers. Until recently, ASCs specialized in providing fairly simple types of surgeries (*e.g.*, knee surgery, colonoscopies) on an outpatient basis, meaning that the patient goes home at the end of the procedure. Because ASCs do not require permanent bed-space, a large staff, emergency room facilities, and the other trappings of full hospital, they generally enjoy relatively lower overhead and cost reductions. As the United States government continues to search for ways to lower Medicare costs, the use of ASCs and other outpatient facilities is expected to grow. Indeed, the scope of the services provided by ASCs also continues to expand, with even some simpler and safer types of heart procedures now being performed on patients who are then sent home at the end of the procedure. As the scope of services expand, so does the capital needs of ASCs in terms of facilities and equipment.

### 3.5.2    Specialty Hospitals

Specialty hospitals fall on the spectrum of healthcare providers somewhere between ASCs and full hospitals. Perhaps partially because of the use of the word "hospital" to describe these organizations, they have been the subject of almost continual controversy since they first debuted in the 1980s. Specialty hospitals have bed space for overnight recovery by patients, but are otherwise limited in the types of services they provide. They do not have emergency rooms, and some simply send their patients to a full-service hospital in the event a patient enters into a life-threatening condition or becomes unstable. Proponents of orthodox hospitals accuse specialty hospitals of cherry-picking the easiest and most profitable procedures, robbing local community hospitals of revenues, inflating their patient outcome data, and exaggerating their cost-savings (by treating only the healthiest patients). The opponents to specialty hospitals even once succeeded in getting legislation passed that effectively banned specialty hospital formation by changing Medicare rules. Such Medicare rules lapsed in August 2006, and since then a few additional specialty hospitals have been formed, but they remain controversial.[11]

Proponents of specialty hospitals claim they achieve high financial and medical efficiency by focusing on particular procedures and/or the treatment of particular body parts or systems. For example, a specialty hospital might focus its entire practice on spinal surgery and spine related ailments. Proponents of specialty hospitals also accuse regular hospitals of waste, inefficiency and of being mistake-prone. In contrast, proponents argue that specialization allows for costs to fall, expertise to improve, and medical mistakes to be eliminated.

---

[11]  Whelan, *Stop that Patient*, at 95.

### 3.5.3 Hospices and Home Healthcare Providers

Home healthcare providers are often regionally or locally based and offer home-based care under the supervision of physicians and nurses. Home healthcare providers are often thought of as a competitor to long term care facilities, as elderly patients elect to stay in their homes or with family members for longer periods of time before needing more comprehensive, facility-based care. Home care can also refer to companies that provide home respiratory and infusion therapy services. Hospice companies provide palliative care and services for terminally ill people (with a life expectancy of six months or less). Hospice care can be provided at the person's home or at a facility. Hospice care focuses on comfort and supportive care, as opposed to cure and treatment. Services rendered by hospice companies include pain management, counseling, medical equipment, and supplies.

### 3.5.4 Management or Service Companies

Healthcare service companies comprise the broad array of companies that provide goods and services to healthcare providers. Healthcare service companies include technology companies, suppliers, management firms, clinical research organizations, claims processing and billing companies, laundry and food service companies, logistics providers, staffing companies, utilization review organizations, and the like. Many healthcare service companies, such as managed care companies, invest heavily in information technology.

### 3.5.5 Complimentary and Alternative Medicine

Complimentary and alternative medicine (CAM) is an overly inclusive term for a great many non-Western healing techniques, including homeopathy, naturopathy, chiropractic care, herbal medicines, and message therapy. While the efficacy of these techniques is much debated and discussed, it is beyond dispute that large numbers of people use them and many payors are beginning to include these types of services as covered services. Research done on the populations of developed countries indicates that "about half the general population… uses complementary and alternative medicine."[12] With demand for such products so high, and with the "pill and scalpel" approach to medicine under sustained cultural attack, it appears likely that a great deal of investment will be made in CAM suppliers in the future.

---

[12] Edzard Ernst, *Obstacles to Research in Complementary and Alternative Medicine*, Medical Journal of Australia, 2003, 179(6): 279–80.

# 4

# Various Financing Concepts and How They Work

## 4.1    Cash Flow Financing

Cash flow financing (often referred to as traditional commercial financing) is focused on the operational cash flow of the borrower as opposed to the value of the borrower's assets. Cash flow financing can be in the form of revolving loan and term loan facilities used by the borrower for a variety of purposes, such as increasing working capital and providing financing for acquisitions and capital expenditures. Cash flow loans may be secured or unsecured depending on the borrower's ability to repay the loans and any restrictions contained in any other credit arrangements of the borrower.

A cash flow lender analyzes a borrower's historical cash flow to ensure the borrower has consistently generated sufficient excess cash to repay its obligations. As part of this analysis, the lender needs to develop a complete understanding of the recurring cash expenses of the borrower, including cash needed to make all scheduled debt payments and planned capital expenditures. Where a borrower intends to have third party credit arrangements in place after the funding of the cash flow loan, the cash flow lender will normally require an intercreditor and/or subordination agreement providing the cash flow lender with various rights, such as the right to be repaid in full prior to repayment of all other lenders and the right to block payments to other lenders in the event the borrower defaults.

As cash flow lenders look to the borrower's operational cash flow for repayment as opposed to the value of the borrower's assets, cash flow lenders traditionally require stringent testing to determine the continuing operational health of the borrower. These tests take the form of financial covenants set forth in the loan documents (examples include fixed charge coverage ratios, interest coverage ratios, leverage ratios, capital expenditure limitations, and minimum earnings requirements). Financial covenants are designed to warn the lender of financial difficulties faced by the borrower. Borrowers are typically required to deliver monthly or more frequent financial covenant compliance certificates to the lender. In the event a borrower fails to satisfy a financial covenant, the borrower will be in default under the loan documents and the lender will be entitled to exercise its remedies. The lender's remedies generally include the right to stop lending, increase interest rates, and sell collateral.

As discussed elsewhere, the nature of a cash-and-carry industry often makes cash flow loans the loan of choice for the healthcare industry, especially for larger and financially healthier borrowers.

## 4.2    Asset-Based Financing

Asset-based financing refers to loans secured by all or certain of the assets of the borrower. Current assets (most often accounts receivable) are usually the primary collateral for revolving loans (and such assets determine the borrower's ability to draw a revolving loan), while fixed assets are usually the primary collateral for term loans. In loan documentation, the borrower will typically pledge all of its assets to the lender (with certain exceptions) as security for the repayment in full of the loans. Prior to determining the loan package made available to the borrower, the lender will usually appraise the value and analyze the liquidity of the borrower's assets. Asset-based loans are typically light on financial covenants but allow for regular inspections and audits of the borrower's assets.

While the amount of a term loan will usually be based on the appraised value of the applicable assets of the borrower at the time of the loan, the availability the borrower has in respect of revolving loans will typically be subject to a borrowing base customarily comprised of 80% eligible accounts receivable and 50% eligible inventory. This arrangement provides liquidity to the borrower for assets that have not yet been converted into cash. The borrower's revolving loan availability is determined on a regular basis through the borrower's delivery of a borrowing base certificate to the lender. The borrowing base certificate is normally completed by the chief financial officer or similar officer of the borrower and delivered to the lender on a monthly or more frequent basis. There are numerous factors that go into the determination of what constitutes "eligible accounts receivable" and "eligible inventory." Only what is considered "eligible" may be borrowed against. For example, in the case of accounts receivable, accounts outstanding for more than 90 days and private pay accounts are generally considered ineligible, and, in the case of inventory, obsolete inventory and inventory not in the possession of the borrower are generally considered ineligible. In addition, lenders generally maintain the right to impose reserves in the borrowing base to take into account changes in the borrower's business. For example, a lender may impose a reserve due to Medicare liabilities or malpractice liability exposure. A reserve provides the lender with additional protection that the loan will not become larger than the collateral securing the loan.

To the extent an asset-based lender is confident that it has properly appraised the value and liquidity of the borrower's assets, the lender need not focus entirely on the overall financial health of the borrower because the assets will provide the source of repayment in the case of a default situation.

## 4.3    Lockbox Lending

Lockbox lending is basically a more expensive but also more secure cousin to asset-based lending. Rather than use a borrowing base mechanism, the borrower and the lender arrange for payments on borrower's accounts receivable to be deposited with a bank or other financial institution. The bank, or lockbox, processes checks and other payments, reports deposits to the borrower, and then either (1) transfers the funds out of the lockbox account to the borrower's discretionary account, or (2) remits the money directly to the lender.

In essence, the lockbox arrangement is a floating escrow arrangement in which borrower gives up the right to have absolute control over its receivables. The lender has the comfort of knowing that it has unilateral recourse to the receivables, without need for any action taken or cooperation from the borrower.

If the money is swept by the lender from the lockbox account, it is used to pay down a revolving loan. That means that extra borrowing power is then freed up for the borrower to once again draw on the revolving loan the next day. While this arrangement provides the lender with maximum security, it still must look to future receivables for complete repayment, especially if the revolver is totally drawn down the day before complete repayment is to be made. For their part, borrowers would prefer to use their own money to finance their operations and only borrow when necessary; an automatic sweep, however, makes every dollar a borrower uses, even from its own operations, a borrowed dollar. On the other hand, the extra security an automatic cash sweep provides to the lender may allow the lender to charge a lower interest rate or enter into a loan it would not have otherwise made.

Financing a borrower's accounts receivable is sometimes structured through an intermediary special purpose vehicle (SPV). The structure is similar in many ways to a lockbox. The provider sells its accounts receivable to the SPV, a separate legal entity created just for this purpose. The purchase price is financed through a loan made by a lender to the SPV. The loan to the SPV, in turn, is secured by the accounts receivable (now owned by the SPV). The SPV may have a charter that prohibits it from incurring other debt, as well as other features that make it "bankruptcy remote." As a result, the lender is able to make a loan to a borrower, *i.e.*, the SPV, that enjoys a higher credit rating and offers less risk than the underlying healthcare provider. This allows the loan to be made at a lower rate of interest. All the while, the provider is the ultimate economic beneficiary of the transaction.

As discussed elsewhere, lockbox lending in the healthcare industry is also complicated by government regulations which make it harder for heathcare borrowers to assign or hypothecate receivables owed by the government.

## 4.4    Real Estate Financing

Real property often is one of the most valuable assets on a healthcare provider's balance sheet. Through real estate financing, the healthcare provider is able to unlock the value of the real property and use loan proceeds to address its capital needs. In the healthcare sector, real estate finance can be employed as a stand-alone source of funds or used in conjunction with the other forms of financings described in this monograph. In most instances, real estate financing is secured by a mortgage on land, facilities, and rents, as applicable.

When real estate finance is used as a stand-alone source of funds, a lender appraises the property based on the income it produces as well as the value of the land and fixtures themselves. The loan is then based on that aggregate value. Depending on the quality and nature of the assets, real estate loans most often have loan-to-value ratios between 60% to 80%, although with many lenders, the permissible loan-to-value ratio is negotiable depending on the interest rate that the borrower is willing to pay.

The financing of medical office buildings is one of the common forms of real estate financing in the healthcare sector. If a hospital owns a medical office building that it leases to doctors, the hospital can obtain a loan based on the rental stream from building. At closing, the hospital would receive a lump sum amount which could be used to refinance the building, perform capital improvements, or for any other purposes, and the lender would receive a mortgage on the building as security for the loan.

During the course of the loan, the hospital will use the rental payments to make interest and amortization payments on the loan.

Another common example of real estate finance is if the hospital is constructing a new facility, a lender could provide the funds for that construction. Generally, construction loans will be at lower loan-to-value ratios than for existing real property and, since the asset will not be producing income during the term of the loan, the lender will want to know in advance how it will be repaid. Repayment can occur by refinancing the property, if the property will produce rental income, or it could occur by the healthcare provider being able to borrow more money from its other sources because it will have a greater ability to render services.

Most often, real estate financing is part of an overall collateral package. In connection with an asset-based loan, a lender may disburse additional funds based on the value of the underlying real property. If the borrower's business should fail, the lender will be able to foreclose on the real property.

## 4.5    Equipment Financing and Capital Leases

The practice of modern medicine requires highly sophisticated and expensive equipment. By late 2007, high-end MRI machines, complete with a warranty and employee training, were coming in package deals costing over $4 million. Healthcare providers that cannot afford such a large capital outlay can often resort to leasing. Leasing (a form of term borrowing) allows for immediate use of expensive equipment in exchange for a stream of payments, each of which is much lower in any given month than payment of the entire purchase price.

An alternative to leasing is secured financing, often vendor financing, in which a hospital or healthcare provider agrees to pay for a piece of equipment over time but receives delivery immediately. The equipment is then operated in a manner to hopefully pay for itself. The future payments are considered debt payments, and the equipment is used as collateral securing the loan. When a single piece of equipment is a major source of collateral, lenders will typically require the borrower to insure that equipment. Similarly, lenders generally want the right to inspect the equipment and have access to the equipment.

Equipment leases typically come in two general forms, one of which is a lease in name only. A *true lease* is one in which the lessor (*i.e.*, the equipment's owner) keeps title to the equipment and actually takes the equipment back after the lease expires. Generally, the equipment has residual value when the lessor takes the equipment back. A *capital lease*, on the other hand, is a disguised form of secured loan. Lease payments under a capital lease are designed to effect a complete payment for the useful life of the machine, just as if it had been purchased, by the end of the lease. The lessee under a capital lease usually has the option of buying the machine at the end of the lease for a nominal amount.

The differences among a true lease, a capital lease, and a secured equipment loan are technical and depend on fine legal and actuarial distinctions. In each case, monthly payments are being exchanged for use of equipment, regardless of what legal label the transaction is given. Nevertheless, the label can have highly significant tax, accounting, and legal consequences. The consequences of a borrower or lessee going into bankruptcy can be especially harsh, depending on whether a leased machine is considered to be the subject of a true lease (keeping it out of the bankruptcy estate) or a disguised financing (creating a creditor right to adequate protection).

## 4.6 HUD Lending

The Department of Housing and Urban Development (HUD) provides mortgage insurance, including construction loans and long term capital, to long term care facilities through its Section 232 program. The HUD Section 232 program insures HUD approved lenders against loss for mortgage defaults. Interest rates on HUD loans are relatively low. The Section 232 program can provide loans with up to 35-year amortization for refinancing. Required loan-to-value for HUD loans is up to 90% (or 95% for non-profit facilities) for new construction and up to 85% (or 90% for non-profit facilities) for refinancing and acquisitions.

## 4.7 FHA Section 242 Mortgage Program

The Federal Housing Administration's Section 242 mortgage insurance program provides lower interest rates and credit enhancement to mortgage debt for a maximum 25-year mortgage term. The Section 242 program supports the financing of new hospitals or capital improvements of facilities. The Federal Housing Administration has approved certain mortgage lenders for these loans. A Federal Housing Administration insured mortgage can cover up to 90% of the replacement of the collateral. Qualification for the Section 242 program generally requires a facility to have positive operating margins.

## 4.8 Construction Loans

A construction loan is a type of real estate loan, where a major part of the collateral securing the loan, a building, is being built with the loan proceeds. If the building never comes into existence, or is only half built by the time all loan proceeds are spent, from a lender's perspective, this consequence may be worse than no collateral at all, since it will require additional outlays to finish. Thus, construction loans, while safer than being unsecured, are nevertheless fairly risky and complicated credits. Lenders must take care to closely monitor construction, create a system of incentives and milestones to ensure timely and on-budget completion of construction, and above all make sure that money is loaned in successive but small amounts and only when a construction timetable requires it.

## 4.9 Sale-Leaseback Arrangements

In a sale-leaseback transaction, a third party purchases a particular project or facility and leases it back to the healthcare provider or a related organization. The purchaser will usually provide an equity component to the investment and borrow the remainder as debt. The tenant receives the proceeds and then leases the project or facility back from the purchaser. The rental payments from the tenant provide the cash flow to repay the debt plus create an equity return for the investor.

## 4.10    Vendor Financing

In its most basic form, vendor financing is simply a loan made by a vendor to its customer, on the condition that the loan be used to purchase the vendor's products. While there may be sound and proper economic reasons for doing this, vendor financing is susceptible to abuse, because it allows the vendor lender to essentially buy its own product, thereby inflating its sales. Often the interest rates charged are higher than might be obtained if the equipment buyer were to obtain a loan from a third party and use the funds to purchase equipment. However, for a borrower with few other options, vendor financing may be the only way to obtain the use of expensive medical equipment. More complicated vendor financing arrangements involve third party lending specialists who provide the capital to the manufacturer to make the loan. Such lenders then take an assignment from the manufacturer of the loan repayment proceeds or a guaranty from the manufacturer that it will repay the loan in the event the equipment's end user defaults. Loans originated by third parties might therefore be made to either the manufacturer or the ultimate equipment user. Either way, the presumption is that the operation of the equipment will enable the user to generate revenue, thereby repaying the loan. Vendor financing may at times blur with more traditional equipment leasing arrangements, as when a third party agrees to purchase the equipment from a manufacturer and then immediately rent it to the ultimate user. Various legal variations on this basic economic structure exist.

## 4.11    Bond Financing

Bonds are a form of long-term financing for capital projects whereby the borrower or, in the case of tax-exempt bonds, a governmental issuer, for the benefit of the borrower, issues notes or other debt instruments commonly called bonds. Bonds can be either taxable or tax-exempt as discussed more fully below. The bonds are sold to investors in a private placement or a limited or general public offering, and the proceeds of the sale of the bonds are used by the borrower to finance its project. By issuing the bonds, the issuer agrees to make principal and interest payments on specific dates to the holders. If the bonds are tax-exempt, they must be issued by a governmental issuer, and taxable bonds may, but need not, be issued by a governmental issuer. If the bond is issued by a governmental issuer, the issuer will loan the proceeds from the sale of the bonds to the borrower and the borrower agrees to repay the loan in amounts and at the times necessary to retire the debt.

### 4.11.1    Tax-Exempt Revenue Bonds

Interest paid on tax-exempt revenue bonds is generally not included in the adjusted gross income of the owner of the bond for federal income tax purposes. Because of the income tax exemption, the interest rates on a tax-exempt bonds are significantly lower than otherwise comparable taxable financing as further described below. The issuance of tax-exempt bonds requires the use of a state or local governmental issuer, typically a municipality or state financing authority. Notwithstanding the fact that a governmental body issues the bonds, the governmental body may not be responsible for repayment or collection, depending on the structure. In many cases, the healthcare provider that received the loan proceeds is solely responsible for repayment of the bonds. The issuer's rights against the borrower are assigned to an indenture trustee.

Tax-exempt financing for healthcare projects is only available to organizations that are exempt from federal income taxation under the Internal Revenue Code (the Code), as described in Section 501(c)(3) of the Code. 501(c)(3) organizations must be organized and operated solely for one or more of religious, charitable, scientific, educational or certain other limited purposes. Projects financed with tax-exempt bonds must be owned *and* used exclusively by a 501(c)(3) organization in furtherance of its exempt purpose, and not in an unrelated trade or business, or be owned and used by a governmental unit. 95% of the proceeds of a tax-exempt financing must be used for land or depreciable property.

### 4.11.2    Taxable Bonds

Taxable financing involves the issuance of bonds or notes, the interest on which is not exempt from federal income tax. Taxable bonds can be issued directly by the borrower without the involvement of a governmental issuer or can be issued by a governmental issuer as a stand-alone issue or in conjunction with the issuance of tax-exempt bonds. Taxable debt financing is an alternative to tax-exempt financing where a borrower or part or all of a project does not qualify for tax-exempt financing. For example, a 501(c)(3) organization may enter into for-profit joint ventures or other strategic initiatives that do not meet its exempt purposes, making taxable debt the only financing option. Unlike tax-exempt financing, taxable financing does not limit a hospital or other healthcare provider in how it uses the proceeds.

### 4.11.3    Taxable or Tax-Exempt

Assuming a borrower and project meet the threshold requirements for tax-exempt financing ((501(c)(3) organization or governmental unit and 95% land and depreciable property) the main consideration in the decision whether a hospital or other healthcare provider should do its financing as tax-exempt financing or as taxable financing is one of cost and flexibility regarding the use of loan proceeds.

The cost savings from a tax-exempt financing are first derived from the fact that bondholders are willing to accept lower interest rates on tax-exempt bonds than they would on comparable taxable debt instruments. Historically, this has meant that the interest rates on tax-exempt hospital bonds of a particular maturity were, on average, approximately 200 basis points (2%) lower than the interest rates on a comparable taxable bond.

In addition to lower interest rates, tax-exempt bonds also offer potential cost savings through certain arbitrage earnings which borrowers can usually derive from the difference between taxable and tax-exempt interest rates. Specifically, certain portions of the bond proceeds can be reinvested for temporary periods, including certain construction periods, in taxable securities, yielding a higher interest rate than the interest rate on the bonds. This provides a certain amount of arbitrage earnings that lowers the effective interest rate to the borrower. In addition, as a general matter, unless donations and other contributions are designated for the project, they can be invested in taxable investments as reserves or an endowment and need not be used to finance the project. Since Internal Revenue Code regulations and rulings governing arbitrage are complex and change from time to time, bond counsel should be consulted about the ways in which arbitrage earnings can be maximized. Violation of arbitrage restrictions can cause interest on the tax-exempt bonds to become taxable retroactively to the date of issuance of the bonds.

Tax-exempt bonds are, however, costlier to issue than taxable bonds. Bond counsel must be employed, the governmental issuer frequently demands a fee, the documents are more complex and longer in a tax-exempt financing than in a non-tax exempt financing, the structure of a tax-exempt financing is much more complicated, and ongoing record keeping and compliance requirements must be observed. Despite these higher costs, the total financing cost to a healthcare entity is almost always less in a tax-exempt bond issue, and up to 2% of bond proceeds can be used to pay issuance costs.

In addition to the interest rate, expedience also affects the decision of whether to pursue taxable or tax-exempt financing. Certain states have detailed requirements for the issuance of tax-exempt bonds which require various filings, hearings, and other time-consuming procedures. The requirements for issuing tax-exempt bonds may include obtaining approval from the local issuer, validation proceedings, and, in certain instances, waiting one's turn in line with the issuing entity in order to go to the market. Taxable financings, however, have much fewer requirements. Thus, if timing of an issuance is a factor, taxable bonds may be favored.

Flexibility of financing terms used to be another factor that affected whether to use taxable or tax-exempt financing. Today, however, both taxable and tax-exempt documents are generally fairly flexible and can be structured to meet the particular needs of a healthcare entity. In certain cases, however, state law or the issuing authority can impose significant limitations on the flexibility of a hospital or healthcare entity to structure its bond issue in the form most advantageous to it. For example, some states prohibit loan agreement financings without a mortgage.

The term and structure of debt payments is another important factor. The market for tax-exempt health facility bonds generally accepts bonds with a term of 30 to 35 years to maturity. The market for taxable bonds, however, accepts bonds with a maximum maturity of only 20 years or less. Additionally, annual debt service payments can be reduced in many taxable and some tax-exempt financings that are 10 years or less by requiring the payment of interest only until the final payment on the loan, at which time all principal, plus the final interest payment, is made in one balloon payment. Thus, a healthcare entity's desired time period for repayment of the bonds may dictate which type of financing is used.

Finally, philosophical considerations may play a part in the decision. Tax-exempt bonds must be issued by a governmental entity in order to comply with federal tax provisions. Yet, some hospitals, particularly religiously affiliated hospitals, may not wish to borrow money through a government entity. Specifically, religiously affiliated hospitals may be concerned that the mere existence of a governmental issuer for the debt could be used to force them to conduct procedures which violate their religious principles. One way to alleviate such concerns is to include a provision in the tax-exempt bond documents permitting the healthcare entity to call the bonds if it is required to perform any procedure or do any other act in contradiction of its moral code or charter.

### 4.11.4    Public Issue or Private Placement

Whether a bond issue is taxable or tax-exempt, the healthcare institution must also choose either a public issue through an underwriter or a private placement with an institutional buyer by a placement agent or underwriter.

Generally, it is difficult to make a private placement at competitive interest rates for an issue over $100 million (unless the issue is rated AAA) due to the limited private placement market. For issues under $100 million, however, a private placement is especially attractive because it permits the healthcare entity to avoid certain substantial front-end costs of a publicly underwritten issue which are less significant when spread over a larger issue. However, the prevalence of private placements have recently increased.[1]

Another factor to consider when choosing between a public issue or a private placement is interest payments. Typically, the interest rate on the bonds sold in a public issue are ⅛ to ¾% lower than in a private placement. The purchaser in a private placement is able to obtain this premium as a trade-off for, among other things, the reduced front-end costs of a private placement.

### 4.11.5    The Bond Indenture

In virtually all public issues, regardless of whether they are tax-exempt or taxable, and in some larger private placements with multiple bond purchasers or participants, the bonds are issued under a trust indenture, and an indenture trustee is appointed to administer the trust and act on behalf of the bondholders. The bond indenture governs the application of the bond proceeds and provides a means for the collection of payments from the borrower on its loan and payments to the bondholders of principal and interest on the bonds from those loan payments. In a tax-exempt issue, the bond indenture serves an additional function in that the governmental issuer will typically assign its interest in the payments to be made by the borrower and any security therefor, to the indenture trustee for the benefit of the bondholders. The indenture sets forth the terms for repayment of the bonds, covenants and defaults, and rights and remedies of the indenture trustee. The ability of the trustee to exercise certain default remedies may be subject to specified percentages of bondholder approval. In this way, the indenture seeks to assure a coordinated approach to enforcement of remedies and equal treatment of bondholders of equal rank. The indenture also governs the application of loan payments and other proceeds.

For example, in a construction project financing, the trustee may be required to deposit from the bond proceeds: (i) an amount equal to the interest to become due on the bonds during the construction period into an interest fund; (ii) an amount equal to the annual debt service requirement in a debt service reserve fund; (iii) an amount to pay fees and expenses incurred in connection with the issuance and sale of the bonds into an expense fund; and (iv) the balance of the proceeds into a construction fund. The trustee under the bond indenture is then required to apply the balance of the bond proceeds (after certain deposits to other funds for interest and issuance expenses) to a construction fund,

---

[1] Modern Healthcare, Sept.1, 2006, *Dealing Direct: Private Placement—still as just a fraction of the debt market— have grown more popular by offering providers speed, flexibility; See also* Healthcare Financial Management, Aug. 2006, *Tax Exempt Private Placements: A new Opportunity for Not-for-Profit Providers.*

the purpose of which is to provide funds sufficient to pay all costs of construction of the project as they become due. If the amount of bond proceeds so deposited is or becomes insufficient for such purpose, the borrower is typically required to make additional deposits into the construction fund so that there will be sufficient moneys to pay all costs of construction when due.

A typical indenture also establishes a number of accounts controlled by the trustee, each with a specific purpose, such as: (i) a revenue fund; (ii) an interest fund; (iii) a bond sinking fund; (iv) a debt service reserve fund; and (v) an optional redemption fund in order to receive funds used to pay the principal of and interest on the bonds.

### 4.12   Mezzanine Financing

Mezzanine financing (often referred to as subordinated debt financing) is typically used by borrowers that are unable to meet their capital needs through traditional senior debt or equity financing. Mezzanine lenders stand midway (*i.e.*, the mezzanine) between the holders of senior debt and equity holders of the borrower. In the event the borrower's financial health deteriorates, the senior debt is repaid first, the mezzanine debt is repaid second, and the equity is left with any remaining residual value. Mezzanine financing may be used for any number of purposes, including financing for acquisitions, recapitalizations, and growth capital. The mezzanine loan market includes lenders of all different shapes and sizes, such as mezzanine divisions of traditional banks able to make mezzanine loans in excess of $50 million and smaller mezzanine funds willing to loan $1 million or more.

As described above, mezzanine debt is riskier in terms of repayment than senior debt. To compensate for the additional risk, mezzanine loans have interest rates that are in excess of the interest rate charged on senior debt. For example, it is not uncommon for a mezzanine lender to charge interest at 14% per annum, with 12% paid in cash on a quarterly basis and the remaining 2% paid-in-kind (*i.e.*, capitalized to principal). In addition, mezzanine lenders often take an equity position in the borrower (or holding company of the borrower) through warrants or an equity co-investment. Even with the higher interest rates and possible equity requirements, mezzanine debt is a useful tool because it can be structured to meet the financial requirements of the borrower.

While mezzanine loans are generally unsecured, in the healthcare finance market, mezzanine lenders typically take a pledge of the borrower's equity as collateral. The equity pledge allows the mezzanine lender, in the case of a default, to control the borrower or sell it as a going concern after the senior debt has been repaid. This aspect may be negotiated with the borrower's senior lender if the senior lender expects to have such pledge itself.

Given the subordinated nature of mezzanine debt, the senior lender and mezzanine lender typically enter into an intercreditor and subordination agreement setting forth restrictions on the payments that are permitted to be made to the mezzanine lender and the right of the senior lender to be repaid in full prior to the repayment of the mezzanine debt.

# 5

# Legal Concepts and Documents Relevant to Most Healthcare Transactions

Before delving into four prototypical deals in **Chapter 6**, the following will highlight the documentation and concepts which come into play in most healthcare financing transactions.

## 5.1  Term Sheet; Commitment

A term sheet or letter of intent is a non-binding expression of interest by a lender to make a loan. Usually, a term sheet is provided without the lender having first received internal credit committee approval to make a loan. The term sheet will broadly summarize the general terms and conditions of the loan, such as the loan amount, type of loan, term, use of proceeds, collateral, interest rate, fees, and some specific deal terms or covenants. The term sheet also contains agreements by the borrower to pay legal and third party fees in connection with the loan. A term sheet is often used by borrowers to compare deal terms among potential lenders. Fees or deposits paid by a borrower to a lender in connection with a term sheet are sometimes refundable if the lender does not proceed with making the loan.

For real estate loans, a loan application is often used in lieu of a term sheet. An application contains detailed provisions regarding the borrower, the loan and some specific loan terms.

A commitment letter, in contrast to a term sheet, is a firm and binding agreement by a lender to make a loan. A commitment letter will contain numerous terms and conditions upon which the lender is obligated to make the loan. The commitment letter sets forth significantly more detail than a term sheet with respect to the proposed loan terms. For instance, a commitment letter sets forth the particular financial covenants, reporting requirements, fees, prepayment terms, syndication requirements, and other material terms. A commitment letter typically states that the loan itself is subject to definitive written agreements as well as other conditions precedent, such as UCC searches, insurance, appraisals, and other due diligence. Some lenders will add general "material adverse change" conditions to commitment letters to protect themselves if changes in the credit market or borrower occur that would cause the lender to reevaluate the loan terms at the time the loan transaction is to occur.

Because the issuance of a commitment letter requires credit approval by an internal credit committee and additional time and expense, some lenders opt to work straight from a term sheet to loan documents. As consideration for this additional time and effort, lenders often require a commitment fee (e.g., 1% of the loan amount) from the borrower for making the commitment. The commitment fee will be deemed earned at the time the commitment letter is issued, whereby other fees would be considered earned at the time the loan is closed, or during the term of the loan. Borrowers are generally required to put down a good faith deposit toward this fee. Since additional fees are involved, borrowers are often more reluctant to request a commitment letter unless one is required. For healthcare loans, borrowers often need a commitment letter for regulatory purposes. For example, in an acquisition of a healthcare facility, the purchaser may need to demonstrate financial capacity for regulatory approval related to the change of control. If the commitment fee is high enough, and the commitment letter requires the borrower to reimburse the lender for its costs, the commitment process creates a financial disincentive for the borrower to find competing lenders who may be willing to make the loan on more favorable terms.

## 5.2     Due Diligence

### 5.2.1     Organizational and Background Checks

Lenders conduct extensive due diligence and background checks in order to know the customer. Lenders will usually review the organizational documents for all borrower and guarantor entities, such as articles of incorporation, good standing certificates, federal tax identification numbers, bylaws, lists of owners, shareholders agreements, operating agreements, and lists of subsidiaries. Lenders also conduct background checks for individual borrowers and guarantors. Pursuant to Executive Order No. 13224, the United States Patriot Act, the Bank Secrecy Act, and regulations promulgated by the U.S. Department of Treasury Office of Foreign Assets Control, lenders are subject to scrutiny in terms of anti-terrorism. Finally, lenders generally review major contracts, subordinated debt documents, intellectual property, bank accounts, insurance, and financial information. Lenders often present borrowers with certificates or questionnaires to complete to obtain the full and accurate corporate information for background check as well as for perfection purposes.

### 5.2.2     UCC, Litigation, Judgment, and Tax Lien Searches

As part of the due diligence process, a lender and its counsel typically conduct UCC, bankruptcy, litigation, judgment, and tax lien searches on the borrower and any guarantor or other credit party. The goal of the searches is to determine the existence of any liens as well as whether the borrower is subject to material litigation and outstanding judgments. Similarly, a lender will usually want to make sure that the borrower has not previously filed bankruptcy. In reviewing UCC search results, a lender may discover UCC financing statements for leased equipment. For healthcare entities, the entry into piecemeal financing transactions funding the purchase of medical equipment, drugs, and supplies is commonplace. Oftentimes, a lien search will find various UCC liens in place on a provider's total asset pool, with each lien staking claim to its own discrete piece of collateral. Lenders and their counsel must carefully review the security grant language to make sure it does not conflict with other financings. Vendors or lessors should have a security interest in the equipment, drugs and supplies as well as proceeds from sale or disposition. Conflicts can arise because income generated by a healthcare entity from the use of equipment, drugs, or supplies would constitute income from business operations and a senior secured lender would expect such amounts to be included in its collateral.

### 5.2.3    Healthcare Diligence

Lenders typically require a healthcare entity to provide a copy of all current licenses, certificates of need, state surveys, notices, complaints, claims, or waivers from federal and state governmental authorities (such as CMS) or other governmental, quasi-governmental, or regulatory agency or accreditation agencies, including any deficiency notices, notices of investigations, or notices of audit. A lender will usually want to confirm that the healthcare entity is a participating provider in the Medicare and Medicaid programs, as applicable. Similarly, a lender will often review a healthcare entity's corporate compliance program and HIPAA compliance. Lenders will typically examine material litigation especially as it relates to patients or residents.

In addition to licensure and compliance matters, most lenders will review forms of residency agreements, management agreements, intercompany agreements, and any operating leases. For life science companies, most lenders will review material licensing, manufacturing, and distribution agreements.

### 5.2.4    Financial Diligence

Most lenders conduct extensive financial due diligence on the borrower. For example, a lender will review financial statements for all borrowers, principals, and guarantors. Lenders will generally want current and historical financial statements, as well as "gap" operating statements and pro forma financial statements. Lenders often conduct a cash flow audit, review bank accounts, and request copies of budgets. For long term care facilities, lenders will typically review census reports, rent rolls, lengths of stays, and information regarding types of residency plans.

### 5.2.5    Collateral Diligence

Lenders typically analyze certain aspects of the collateral by commissioning and reviewing various reports and analyses. For example, a lender will review bank account information and conduct appraisals, property condition reports, environmental reports, and zoning reports. Most lenders will also make at least one physical site visit.

## 5.3    Structure of the Transaction

As a general matter, the means in which a healthcare provider is structured is highly dependent upon the regulatory framework within which the healthcare provider operates. It is imperative for lenders and their counsel to understand the healthcare industry and healthcare regulatory matters in order to understand the healthcare entity's revenue and assets as collateral. Many healthcare entities have bifurcated structures in which a separate licensed operating entity receives all or a majority of the revenues from operations. These revenues are then often distributed to affiliated and non-affiliated entities through management fees, lease payments, consulting fees, preferred returns, and other distributions. Many life science companies have off-shore operations or hold intellectual property off-shore. Accordingly, lenders must carefully "follow the money" and understand the underlying regulatory environment to include the actual operating revenue as pledged collateral and the proper operating entity as the borrower. Similarly, management fees and fees paid to affiliated parties should be analyzed to determine whether such payments should be specifically subordinated.

In acquisition financing transactions, a lender and its counsel must understand how to structure the financing in light of various change-of-ownership requirements. As discussed above, a change of ownership may require state licensing agency approval, potentially a new certificate of need or a certificate of exemption, and CMS approval with respect to Medicare and Medicaid provider numbers. Due to the difficulty in obtaining all approvals and finalizing transitional matters, many sale transactions are accomplished with the seller or prior operator involved with operations post-closing. For example, a buyer may purchase the underlying real estate and lease the facility back to the licensed operator during such time as the new operator is awaiting all necessary licenses and approvals. The prior operator continues to operate the facility, including billing and collecting revenues. Accordingly, the loan transaction may involve the inclusion of the seller as a credit party, a recorded assignment of leases, as well as a collateral assignment of an operations transfer agreement, including a pledge of post-closing receivables. The same structure may be used in sales of life science companies or other types of licensed healthcare entities. Also, in any acquisition financing, the buyer may have purchased certain seller accounts receivable as part of the transaction. Accordingly, lenders and their counsel must analyze these aspects of the transaction in properly securing the collateral of the loan.

## 5.4    Credit Agreement/Loan Agreement

The credit agreement (or loan agreement) is the comprehensive, definitive agreement governing the loan. In general, the credit agreement begins with a comprehensive set of definitions then addresses the terms and conditions for the loan. The credit agreement addresses the administration of the loan, including whether there is an agent acting on behalf of a syndicate of lenders. The credit agreement will also state the use of proceeds. Careful consideration is given to the use of proceeds to ensure that the proceeds are actually used by and for the benefit of the borrower to avoid fraudulent conveyance issues.

The borrower or borrowers also make a series of representations and warranties to the lender to assure the lender that the facts that the lender is relying upon in making the loan are, in fact, true and remain unchanged. The representations and warranties will require the borrower to make certain disclosures in the event that particular representations and warranties cannot be truthfully made without further explanation. It behooves the borrower to disclose all facts that might make a representation or warranty untrue on the attached schedules attached to the credit agreement. Once disclosed, they can no longer form the basis for a default premised upon the untruth of the representation or warranty. During the course of negotiating the representations and warranties, most borrowers attempt to qualify the representations and warranties upon the borrower's "knowledge" or based upon certain materiality qualifiers. Many lenders resist such language, requiring full and complete disclosure.

The credit agreement will also contain various affirmative and negative covenants with respect to specific matters that the borrower will do or refrain from doing during the course of a loan. Specifically, a credit agreement for a healthcare borrower typically contains an exhaustive regulatory section incorporating representations, warranties, and covenants tailored to the particular healthcare entity and industry. For example, a loan agreement with a skilled nursing facility will contain certain provisions relating to licenses, CONs, licensed beds, HIPAA compliance, accreditations, Medicare and Medicaid participation and billing practices, survey deficiencies, fraud and abuse, resident/admissions agreements, and corporate compliance. The borrower may be subject to specific affirmative and negative covenants. For instance, a borrower may be subject to a prohibition or limitation on the incurrence of additional indebtedness, liens, leases, types of investments, transactions with affiliates, change in business, creation of new subsidiaries, distributions, and sale of assets. The credit agreement will usually contain specific financial covenants that the borrower must meet during the term of the loan.

Finally, the credit agreement typically contains (a) a specific grant of security interests by the borrower in its collateral to the lender,[1] if the financing is secured, (b) closing conditions to the loan, and (c) defaults and remedies. In negotiating the default and remedy provisions, borrowers will generally request specific notice and cure periods for defaults and limitations on the lender's ability to call a default to objective and material standards. Not surprisingly, lenders tend to take the opposite view. Defaults are generally triggered by non-payment, breaches of representations, warranties and covenants, bankruptcy and insolvency, regulatory non-compliance, and material adverse changes in the borrower's financial condition or operations. The borrower will usually also indemnify the lender from any liabilities or damages incurred by the lender as a result of making the loan to the borrower. Similarly, the borrower will generally agree to be responsible for all fees, costs, and expenses incurred in connection with the loan.

In real estate transactions, some lenders used to forgo a credit agreement and instead incorporate all of the loan terms into the mortgage. However, because the mortgage is a public, recorded document, most lenders elect instead to keep the details of its loan in a separate, private document. For real estate loans in the healthcare industry, this practice is especially relevant since the loan will contain many specific regulatory terms.

## 5.5    Promissory Note

While the substantive content of a promissory note can be included in the credit agreement, most lenders prefer a separate promissory note. Conceptually, lenders like the idea of being able to walk into court with a short, simple instrument evidencing the borrower's payment obligation. Since the promissory note is often a negotiable instrument, borrowers should only sign one original copy.

## 5.6    Legal Opinions

In addition to obtaining representations and warranties from the borrower under the credit agreement, a lender will typically require an opinion from the borrower's counsel relating to certain legal matters.[2] Conceptually, the exercise of providing the opinion shifts a due diligence obligation to the borrower's counsel. Sometimes the borrower's counsel is not licensed in the same state in which the loan documents are governed. Depending upon the lender and the deal type and size, a lender may let

---

[1] The Credit Agreement will specifically describe the assets that are the subject of the security interest. In many transactions, collateral matters are documents under a separate security or pledge agreement.

[2] An alternative to obtaining an opinion from the borrower's counsel—or in addition to such opinion—is the purchase of UCC insurance. UCC insurance offers indemnity coverage to the lender. UCC insurance is similar to the title insurance offered on real estate and insures the lender that it has a perfected and prior security interest in its collateral in accordance with the terms of the policy.

such counsel assume that the laws of the state in which the counsel is licensed is the same as the state under which the documents are governed. An opinion from the borrower's counsel will usually cover the following areas[3]:

### 5.6.1    Due Incorporation and Qualification

Borrower's counsel will opine that the borrower is duly incorporated and validly existing under the laws of the state of its incorporation and any other jurisdictions where it is doing business.

### 5.6.2    Power and Authority

Borrower's counsel will opine that the borrower has the corporate power and authority to enter into the loan, to borrow the money, and to enter into and perform the loan documents. The borrower's counsel should verify that all necessary consents have been received in order to provide this opinion.

### 5.6.3    Validity and Perfection

Borrower's counsel usually opines that the financing statements are in proper form and either have been filed in the appropriate jurisdiction under the UCC or, when filed in the appropriate jurisdiction, will perfect a security interest in those assets which can be perfected by the filing of a financing statement. This opinion is typically limited with language indicating that perfection is achieved by the filing of a financing statement. A borrower's counsel does not opine on the priority of the lender's security interest. In giving the opinion, the borrower's counsel will usually assume that the borrower has rights in the collateral and the lender is giving value.

### 5.6.4    No Conflict

Borrower's counsel may opine and confirm that entering into and performing the loan documents will not conflict with or cause a default under any other agreement or document by which the borrower is bound.

### 5.6.5    Binding Effect

Borrower's counsel opines that the loan documents are binding and enforceable against the borrower, subject to multiple exceptions. These include bankruptcy and insolvency proceedings, equitable remedies, and exceptions geared to particular state law.

### 5.6.6    No Litigation

The borrower's counsel generally opines that, to the knowledge of the borrower's counsel's firm, the borrower is not subject to any litigation except as disclosed. The opinion may rely on specific litigation searches.

---

[3] *See* **Appendices C** and **D** for example opinions.

### 5.6.7 No Governmental Consent

The lender may require the borrower's counsel to opine that the execution of and performance of the loan documents does not require governmental consent under federal or state law.

### 5.6.8 Regulatory Opinion

The lender may ask for certain regulatory opinions. For example, the borrower (i) is duly qualified to own and operate the healthcare facility, or its business, as the case may be, (ii) has all licenses, permits, certificates, approvals, or authorizations necessary to use and operate the healthcare facility or its business, and all such licenses are in full force and effect; (iii) a certificate of need application and approval is/is not required for the use and operation of the healthcare facility (as applicable); and (iv) has not received any notices of violations of applicable healthcare laws.

### 5.6.9 Reliance

Lenders will require an opinion to be delivered for its benefit along with the benefit of its successors and assigns, including any purchaser of the loan or any participants to the loan, as well as any rating agencies. Borrower's counsel, in issuing the loan, will indicate that no other party, other than indicated, can rely on the opinion and that the opinion is only rendered as of the date of such opinion letter.

## 5.7 Deposit Account Control Agreements

In order to perfect its security interest in a borrower's deposit account, a lender will require an agreement with the borrower's bank. Such agreement will provide the lender with a lockbox or control over the accounts. Some lockbox agreements include a standing order by the borrower for the bank to transfer funds received into the borrower's deposit account to an account controlled by the lender. As described above, for accounts involving governmental receivables, the deposit account control agreement will include specific language indicating that the healthcare entity has sole dominion and control over the deposit account, but not sweep or lockbox account. The agreement may employ a "double lockbox" function whereby the funds are swept daily from the account in which the healthcare entity maintains control to another account over which the lender has control. Many lenders have pre-negotiated forms of deposit account control agreements with certain banks. To the extent a healthcare entity is utilizing a bank that is not familiar with deposit account control agreements involving healthcare receivables, a lender may require the healthcare entity to switch banks.

## 5.8 Pledge Agreements

Healthcare entities often have licenses and permits that are not transferable. These licenses and permits are generally valuable as an essential aspect of a borrower's business. Accordingly, lenders often require the owners of healthcare borrowers to pledge their ownership interests in the borrower as additional collateral. While lenders often take a pledge of ownership interest in a borrower to facilitate access to that borrower's licenses and permits, lenders are reluctant to realize on such pledge, since lenders generally do not want to actually own licensed healthcare providers. Similarly, while licenses and permits are not transferable, regulatory or licensing bodies generally require prior approval for any change of ownership. Accordingly, the realization of a pledge often requires certain regulatory procedural steps.

### 5.8.1    Stock

If the pledged equity involves stock, the lender will require the borrower to deliver the original stock certificates along with executed blank stock powers. Generally, as long as no event of default has occurred, the stockholders are able to continue to exercise all powers of a stockholder, *i.e.*, vote and receive dividends.

### 5.8.2    LLC Interests

Limited liability company (LLC) interest can either be certificated or uncertificated. If LLC interests are certificated, interests in the LLC are usually in the form of units (as opposed to shares for a corporation). In most cases, LLC membership interests constitute "general intangibles." A security interest in general intangibles is perfected by filing a UCC-1 financing statement. However, LLC interests may not be afforded the same perfection under Article 9 of the UCC with respect to other intangibles in which a secured party may attach and perfect a security interest despite a contractual or legal restriction on the assignment of such assets. In fact, some states such as Delaware and Virginia have specifically revised the UCC provision to exclude LLC interests from the class of general intangibles in which a security interest may attach and be subjected notwithstanding prohibitions on assignment. Many operating agreements contain specific language prohibiting the assignment, transfer or pledge of LLC interests. Accordingly, lenders must conduct a proper review of the LLC operating agreement. If consent to assignment, transfer, or pledge is required, lenders will require such consent as a prerequisite to the loan (assuming the pledge of LLC interested is mandated by the loan terms).

Alternatively, the issuer of securities can "opt in" to Article 8 of the UCC by specifying that the LLC interests are securities governed by Article 8 of the UCC. If the company elects to opt in to Article 8 of the UCC, certain language is required for such option to be effective and, if certificates are issued, the certificates should contain a legend indicating the certificates represent securities that are to be governed under Article 8 of the UCC. The lender will also require language in a pledge agreement that the borrower will not opt out of Article 8 of the UCC. If such actions are properly taken, the security interest in the LLC interests will no longer be treated as a general intangible under Article 9 of the UCC, and, instead, will be treated as an Article 8 security. A lender can then perfect its security interest in the Article 8 security through filing, possession, or control. If the LLC interests are certificated, the lender will take possession of the certificates evidencing the pledged security and an endorsement executed in blank. Alternatively, the parties may enter into a control agreement if the interests are not certificated. A security interest in a security perfected by control or possession usually has priority over a competing security interest that was previously perfected by filing only. Many lenders will also include the LLC interests in a UCC-1 filing even if the lender has possession or control.

### 5.9 Landlord Waivers

Where a borrower leases its facility or facilities at which a lender's collateral is maintained, a lender may require a waiver from the borrower's landlord. The waiver will provide that the landlord waives any claim to the lender's collateral and that the lender will have access to the premises to be able to inspect and remove the collateral.

### 5.10 Commonly Negotiated Loan Provisions

#### 5.10.1 Lender Discretion

As a general matter, lenders will want to reserve certain rights and have a certain amount of discretion. For example, lenders will want the right to set the base rate for any floating rate loan, establish a loan account, conduct audits and site visits, impose borrowing base reserves, limit subordinated debt and other liens, restrict activities outside the ordinary cause of business, and the like. Borrowers, on the other hand, will want to operate their businesses without substantial oversight from lenders and will want to limit the types of matters for which the borrower will need to seek lender approval. Tension arises between the parties as to the nature of the relationship going forward. Unless the lender and borrower have worked together in the past, the lender may not trust the borrower or feel secure in its position. Similarly, the borrower may not feel as though the lender is easy to work with and understanding of its business needs. Borrowers sometimes are particularly wary since the people representing the lender at the time the loan is being made will often be different from the lender employees that manage the loan on an ongoing basis.

#### 5.10.2 Change of Control/Permitted Transfers

Loan agreements typically impose some limitations on a change of control with respect to the ownership of a borrower. At most, a lender may allow transfers up to 49% of a borrower's ownership interest, provided the borrower has complied with the lender's background and anti-terrorism provisions. Lenders will generally allow carve-outs for estate planning purposes.

#### 5.10.3 Material Adverse Effect/Material Adverse Change

The phrase "material adverse effect" is generally used to qualify certain representations, warranties, or covenants. For example, a borrower may want to qualify its representation that it is in full compliance with all regulatory requirements, except where failure to do so would not have a material adverse effect, as such term is defined (and negotiated) in the agreement. The concept of material adverse change arises in the default provisions. Lenders often want the ability to call a default upon a material adverse change in the borrower or its operations. This language and the associated defined terms are often highly negotiated.

### 5.10.4 Permitted Distributions

Lenders often want to limit a borrower's ability to make distributions or dividends to its equity holders, instead preferring that excess cash be left in the borrower, thereby increasing the lender's collateral. For limited liability company or s-corporation borrowers, lenders generally make exception for tax distributions.

### 5.10.5 Payment Grace Periods

Borrowers often request a grace period for payment on the loan. A grace period is common for real estate loans. However, a grace period is not common for revolving loans because the lender has control over the borrower's cash.

### 5.10.6 Reserves/Escrows

Lenders often establish certain reserves or escrow funds. If a lender is holding a borrower's funds, borrowers often request that these sums earn interest. For real estate financings, escrowed reserves for real property taxes and insurance premiums are common. Similarly, real estate financings may also involve holdbacks or reserves capital improvements, capital replacement, and/or unit reservations. A lender may also impose cash collateral accounts to serve as additional collateral. As mentioned previously, some states have also imposed a debt service and operating reserve on certain types of healthcare facilities.

### 5.10.7 Representations, Warranties, and Covenants

Every loan agreement contains a set of representation and warranties addressing fundamental information regarding the borrower and its business. For example, the borrower will represent and warrant to the lender that: (a) it is duly organized, validly existing, and in good standing in the laws of the jurisdiction in which it is formed; (b) it is authorized to enter into the loan and execute the loan documents, and such loan documents are binding upon the borrower; (c) it has provided accurate financial information; (d) it is not the subject of any material or undisclosed litigation; (e) it owns its property and its property is not subject to liens, except as permitted by the lender; (f) it is not in default or in breach with respect to material agreements; (g) it is in compliance with applicable laws; (h) it has filed all taxes due; (i) it is solvent; (j) the interest rate does not violate usury laws; and (k) it has fully disclosed information requested by the lender and the information disclosed is accurate, true, and correct. The borrower and its counsel will typically negotiate these provisions often by qualifying the representations and warranties by materiality or knowledge or through creating various carve-outs or exceptions.

Covenants cover agreements by the borrower to affirmatively do (or not do) certain things during the term of the loan. For example, the borrower will covenant to: (a) provide certain financial information at specified times; (b) pay its obligations and liabilities; (c) comply with the terms of material contracts; (d) maintain its property and existence; (e) comply with law; (f) provide the lender with notices of litigation; and (g) allow for audits and site visits by the lender. With respect to negative covenants, a borrower will covenant not to: (a) incur additional debt, except for certain permitted debt or payables in the ordinary course of business; (b) permit other liens on the lender's collateral; (c) make certain distributions or dividends, except as permitted by the lender; (d) take actions other than in the ordinary course of business; (e) incur any change in control; or (f) modify certain documents.

### 5.10.8    Financial Covenants

Lenders to healthcare entities measure and monitor various financial metrics in connection with a loan. For example, a lender may monitor a healthcare entity's liquidity by assessing cash on hand. The current ratio, debt service coverage ratio, and the length of time an accrual sits as an account receivable or account payable provides information as to an entity's current financial health. A liquidity decline, such as a drop in cash reserves, decrease in days of cash on hand, and extended vendor payments can signal a financial crisis. Similarly, a significant increase in bad debt expense and poor financial reporting can signal trouble ahead. Lenders will usually also look at a healthcare entity's capital structure through indicators such as debt to cash flow, long-term debt to equity, or asset turnover ratio. The following are some typical financial covenants utilized in healthcare loans:

#### 5.10.8.1    Debt Service Coverage Ratio

The debt service coverage ratio is the ratio of a borrower's EBITDA or operating cash flow to the borrower's debt service obligations. A debt service coverage ratio of less than 1 means a negative cash flow.

#### 5.10.8.2    Debt Yield

Debt yield is the percentage obtained by dividing a borrower's operating cash flow by debt service.

#### 5.10.8.3    Current Ratio

The current ratio measures current assets divided by current liabilities. The current ratio evaluates a borrower's liquidity or ability to meet short term debts. Generally, a minimum acceptable current ratio is 1:1. Lenders may want to include the loan amount in the definition of current liabilities, even if the loan will not be due for a few years, so that a borrower cannot borrow its way into compliance with a current ratio test.

#### 5.10.8.4    Fixed-Charge Coverage Ratio

The fixed-charge coverage ratio measures profits before income tax and interest payments (and/or lease expenses) divided by long-term interest and/or other fixed charges (such as lease expenses). The ratio indicates the risk involved in the borrower's ability to pay fixed financing expenses if business declines.

### 5.10.8.5  Measurement Periods

The demonstration of compliance with financial covenants can be time-consuming and burdensome for borrowers. Lenders often have compliance certificates to be completed, along with various worksheets and other reporting requirements. Accordingly, borrowers will usually want to reduce the frequency of financial covenant measurements. Monthly measurement periods are common in loans where the lender is closely monitoring a company's ability to repay the debt. Quarterly measurement periods are more common.

### 5.10.9  Prepayment

Lenders generally require prepayment of the loan equal to the net proceeds from any material sale or disposition of assets. Similarly, lenders may require borrowers to apply insurance proceeds toward prepayment of the loan, especially if such proceeds are intended to compensate the borrower for a casualty related to assets that constituted the lender's collateral.

Lenders often impose a prepayment fee upon early prepayment of the loan. Initially the loan may be subject to a lockout, such that the borrower is unable to prepay the loan. Thereafter, the loan may be subject to a percentage exit fee to reimburse the lender for having made the funds available to the borrower. Some lenders will also impose a "make whole" provision to compensate the lender for the loss of the interest it would have earned on that loan. A borrower may be required to pay the difference between the yield on U.S. treasuries and the yield on the loan.

### 5.10.10  Events of Default

Common events of default are non-payment, breach of a representation, warranty or covenant, bankruptcy, failure of the lien to be a perfected lien, ERISA liability, change in control, and specified cross defaults. The following highlights some of the more negotiated provisions:

### 5.10.10.1  Notice and Cure Periods

Borrowers often request notice and opportunities to first cure a default before a lender can take action. With respect to payment defaults, a lender may not agree to a payment grace period when payments are being made on an auto-debit basis. A lender may also be reluctant to agree to provide a borrower notice prior to a default, instead providing for an automatic default, if the lender would not necessarily be in a position to know of the default. For example, if the borrower failed to meet a financial covenant as of a certain date, failed to maintain insurance, or impermissibly distributed dividends, the lender would not have knowledge or provide notice and an opportunity to cure. Usually certain cure periods will be allowed for defaults related to other indebtedness or judgments imposed. Similarly, a period of time may be granted to allow for the dismissal of any involuntary bankruptcy proceeding. Whether a material adverse change default provision is included is generally a heavily negotiated provision. Since the healthcare industry is heavily regulated, healthcare lenders are often more insistent on material adverse change provisions since the borrower's business is more susceptible to volatility. With respect to cure periods, a lender may want to limit the number of times a borrower is allowed to cure a default. For example, once a borrower has cured the same default twice in a 12-month period, a lender may reserve the right to call an immediate default upon the next occurrence without having to wait for another cure period.

### 5.10.10.2  Third Party Loans, Liens, and Judgments

Lenders often impose a "cross" default with other debt of the borrower. In the event the borrower fails to timely its other debt, it can trigger a breach of the loan agreement. The borrower will typically negotiate some limitations on this type of provision by limiting it to "financial indebtedness" and not trade debt, limiting it to acceleration as opposed to default, and including cure periods, dollar thresholds, and the ability to contest the obligation.

### 5.10.10.3  Material Adverse Change Clause

Lenders generally like the flexibility to call a default upon any material adverse change. However, borrowers are reluctant to provide lenders with such broad discretion. If the lender refuses to delete a material adverse change default provision, borrowers usually can negotiate some limitations. For example, a borrower with numerous divisions or properties can define the material adverse change with respect to the business on a whole.

### 5.10.10.4  Default Rate of Interests

A loan agreement typically provides for an increased interest rate upon an event of default by anywhere from an additional 2% to 5%. The imposition of a higher default interest rate is often in addition to a late payment charge.

### 5.10.11  Confession of Judgment

A confession of judgment clause is an agreement whereby the borrower consents to the lender entering a judgment against it. The borrower essentially contracts away its right to raise defenses. The enforceability of confession of judgment clauses varies from state to state. Borrowers often contest any inclusion of a confession of judgment clause in a loan agreement or promissory note. Many lenders have elected to not include such provisions or will negotiate the deletion provided that the overall credit risk warrants it.

### 5.10.12  Financial Reporting and Audits

Loan agreements typically require regular financial reporting from borrowers. Borrowers will generally be obligated to provide the lender with annual, audited financial statements within at least 90 to 120 days after the fiscal year end. Borrowers must also submit monthly or quarterly internally prepared consolidated and consolidating financial statements within 30 to 45 days after month or quarter end. For revolving loans secured by receivables, borrowers need to submit regular borrowing base certificates and monthly aging reports. Lenders may impose other reporting requirements such as budgets, notice of litigation, and other identified items as may be requested by the lender. Lenders reserve the right to conduct audits or field exams. Often, borrowers will negotiate to limit the number of audits the borrower is required to reimburse the lender for, as long as no event of default exists.

### 5.10.13 Fees

For revolving loans, lenders usually charge an unused line fee to compensate a lender for making funds available. Lenders often also charge late fees in addition to default interest. Other common fees are audit fees, exit fees, prepayment fees, and wire fees. For larger transactions, fees may be set forth in a separate fee letter.

## 5.11 Post-Default Complications Unique to Healthcare

Lenders obtain collateral and numerous contractual rights in order to protect against the prospect that the borrower will fail to pay or otherwise default under the agreement. As discussed above, the loan agreement contains a list of things that a borrower is not supposed to do (events of default) as well as a list of rights and remedies that a lender may exercise if the borrower does not perform. One such remedy is the ability to liquidate collateral and use the proceeds to pay off the loan. Other remedies may include the right to file a law suit, to have a receiver appointed, to seize or set-off against money belonging to the borrower, to refuse to lend additional money, and to charge default interest.

### 5.11.1 Traditional Remedies upon Default

Once a default occurs, creditors have a number of legal and contractual remedies available to them. Secured creditors are obviously in a better position to recover than unsecured creditors. In the healthcare industry, as opposed to many other industries, the value of the collateral (*e.g.*, a medical facility) is generally greater if the facility continues to operate as a going concern, as opposed to being liquidated. Simplistically, the value of a medical provider comes from the income stream generated from accounts receivable, the licenses, and provider numbers held by the provider and community goodwill, which generates referrals to the provider. To preserve the going concern value and to address public policy concerns, healthcare facilities are generally left operational. This aspect causes lenders as well as courts to treat healthcare facilities differently from other types of entities or collateral.

Many sales, repossessions, or other enforcement actions by a lender have real estate implications. Real estate foreclosures are governed by state and county law and, unlike foreclosures for personal property, there is no uniformity of the law. Foreclosures on personal property, on the other hand, are generally governed by Article 9 of the UCC. If the lender is willing to take the collateral in full satisfaction of the debt, and not seek to collect any deficiency from the borrower, that is known as a strict foreclosure and it is generally a more streamlined foreclosure process. Foreclosures generally require public notice. Since healthcare facilities are very localized in nature and the success of healthcare facilities often rests highly with community reputation, foreclosures can have a negative effect on the ongoing value and reputation of the facility.

Other alternatives exist to foreclosure or bankruptcy. For instance, the borrower may make an assignment for the benefit of creditors, in which a trustee is appointed and the assets are distributed to creditors. Also, a receiver may be appointed to operate the business and distribute funds at the direction of a court. These alternatives may also be unpalatable to a lender, because they place control over the business in the hands of a third party.

Creditors may also force a debtor into bankruptcy. Under section 303(b) of the Bankruptcy Code[4], three creditors who have claims totaling $13,475 can file an involuntary bankruptcy case against a debtor. If a debtor has fewer than 12 total creditors, just one creditor can file the involuntary bankruptcy. It should be noted that the decision to force a borrower into bankruptcy should not be taken lightly and will require carrying a burden of proof as to various legal elements. The statute provides for costs, fees, and even punitive damages to be assessed against those who try but fail to force a debtor into bankruptcy.[5]

Most healthcare bankruptcies are Chapter 11 filings, which are restructurings, as opposed to Chapter 7 filings, which are liquidations. However, Chapter 11 restructurings can be difficult for lenders since they permit borrowers to continue to operate the business and often continue to use the lenders' cash collateral. If all of the parties are amicable, the debtor and the creditors can often reduce the considerable costs and time spent in a bankruptcy by agreeing on a plan of reorganization before the bankruptcy case is commenced.

The filing of bankruptcy creates an automatic stay that generally enjoins creditors from engaging in a variety of activities directed at the debtor or property of the bankruptcy estate,[6] including the enforcement of a pre-bankruptcy judgment, the collection of pre-bankruptcy claim, the setoff of a pre-petition debt, or the termination of pre-bankruptcy contracts with the debtor.[7] The Bankruptcy Code also empowers a trustee or debtor-in-possession to avoid certain pre-bankruptcy transfers that constitute either voidable preferences or fraudulent transfers.[8]

A bankruptcy filing presents challenges for creditors, including lenders. In order to exercise remedies against the borrower, such as commencing a foreclosure action or effecting a setoff, the lender must first obtain relief from the automatic stay.[9] Pursuant to Bankruptcy Code Section 362(d), upon a request by a party-in-interest (*i.e.*, a non-debtor) and after notice and a hearing, a bankruptcy court may grant relief from the automatic stay for "cause," including the lack of adequate protection of an interest in property.[10]

Disputes can arise in bankruptcy regarding whether the debtor can utilize the lender's cash collateral for operations. The Bankruptcy Code defines cash collateral as "cash, negotiable instruments, documents of title, securities, deposit accounts, or other cash equivalent whenever acquired in which the estate and an entity other than the estate have an interest."[11] Section 363(c)(2) provides that the trustee or debtor-in-possession may not use, sell or lease cash collateral without either the consent of the creditor with an interest in the collateral or court authorization, granted after notice and a hearing.

---

[4] The Bankruptcy Code is set forth in Title 11 of the United States Code, 11 U.S.C. §§ 101–1532.

[5] 11 U.S.C. § 303(i).

[6] *See* 11 U.S.C. § 541 (broadly describing the scope of the property of the bankruptcy estate).

[7] *See* 11 U.S.C. § 362(a).

[8] *See* 11 U.S.C. §§ 547, 548.

[9] *See* 11 U.S.C. § 362(d).

[10] *See* 11 U.S.C. § 361 (describing the basis for adequate protection). Adequate protection, as prescribed under Bankruptcy Code Section 361, affords a secured creditor protection from the depreciation, deterioration or diminution in the value of its collateral as of the date the bankruptcy petition is filed. *See* 11 U.S.C. § 361(1); *Travelers Life Insurance and Annuity Co. v. Ritz-Carlton of D.C., Inc. (In re Ritz-Carlton of D.C. Inc.)*, 98 B.R. 170, 173 (S.D.N.Y. 1989).

[11] 11 U.S.C. § 363(a).

If the lender does not consent, a debtor will seek bankruptcy court approval to use cash collateral on a non-consensual basis and litigate the issue of whether the lender's interests are adequately protected within the meaning of the Bankruptcy Code.

Use of cash collateral alone, however, is often insufficient to satisfy the debtor's cash needs over the course of a Chapter 11 proceeding. Therefore, Bankruptcy Code Section 364 authorizes the debtor to borrow money after the commencement of the case on a super priority, senior secured basis.[12] The pre-petition lender may be required to make such a loan, in order to prevent the healthcare borrower from shuttering. If the lender refuses to do so, the debtor can seek a priming (*i.e.*, senior secured) loan from another lender. Once again, this would trigger litigation regarding whether the pre-petition lender's interests are adequately protected within the meaning of the Bankruptcy Code.

A bankruptcy filing can also raise complex valuation issues, which can arise in the context of a Chapter 11 plan or the allowance of a secured claim. Pursuant to Bankruptcy Code Section 506(a), a creditor with a security interest in the debtor's property is deemed to hold an allowed secured claim in an amount up to the value of the collateral.[13] Where the value of the collateral is not sufficient to pay the entire claim, then the creditor is seen as having two claims in the bankruptcy case: (1) a secured claim, to the extent of the value of the collateral; and (2) an unsecured claim, to the extent that there is a deficiency in the value of the collateral. Where the value of the collateral exceeds the entire claim, the lender is oversecured. Under Bankruptcy Code Section 506(b), an oversecured creditor is generally entitled to post-petition interest and expenses.[14] Such amounts, if not paid, are added to the secured claim.

Bankruptcy issues become particularly complicated when healthcare providers are involved. The various regulatory requirements, licenses, provider numbers, certificates of need, and other permits need to be evaluated in any Chapter 11 plan. Any assumption of an existing Medicaid or Medicare provider number or provider agreement requires careful analysis and coordination among governmental agencies. Assumption of any previous owner's Medicare or Medicaid provider number should be considered only after careful analysis of the legal implications, the liabilities assumed and the operational issues associated with such assumption.

Healthcare facilities also maintain patient lists and medical records which must be handled in accordance with the applicable privacy protections. Generally, when an entity attempts to sell its patient list in bankruptcy, it can sell only its interest in the list, subject to any and all restrictions imposed on the list prior to the bankruptcy filing. So while a patient list is an asset and may be transferred, it is still subject to the same privacy restrictions placed on the selling company. As such, patient lists and patients' medical records may be able to be transferred only as part of the company's goodwill and not as a stand-alone asset.

---

[12] *See* 11 U.S.C. § 364(c). Bankruptcy Code Section 364(c) permits a debtor to obtain secured financing and/or to confer an administrative expense priority claim senior to all administrative expenses of the kind specified in Bankruptcy Code Sections 503(b) or 507(b); *i.e.*, a so-called "superpriority" administrative expenses claim.

[13] 11 U.S.C. § 506(a).

[14] *See* 11 U.S.C. § 506(b).

### 5.11.2    Reasons Why Traditional Remedies May Not Always Work in the Healthcare Context

In the healthcare context, and especially so in the case of active hospitals and nursing care facilities filled with patients, typical secured creditor remedies may be unpalatable. Patient care issues, the ability to assign licenses, and the need to preserve the going concern value of the borrower's operations also can limit a lender's options.

#### 5.11.2.1    *Patient Care*

Given issues related to patient care, it is simply not possible to close down a hospital or a nursing care facility overnight or even during the span of several months. Regulatory bodies or agencies often step in to prevent such outcomes. Many states impose certain debt service and operating reserve requirements specifically to prevent closures of facilities. Upon a default, those reserves are utilized to continue operations and make debt service payments.

#### 5.11.2.2    *Maintaining Going Concern Value*

Healthcare management and administration is complex, and replacement managers have to contend with an unknown, distressed situation which potentially exposes them to liability. Most financial institutions have limited to no expertise in running healthcare entities, nor are they interested in the risks and potential liabilities involved in direct operation. Moreover, the liquidation of a healthcare provider, as with any other service business, would destroy the going concern value. Indeed, the best economic decision may very well be to advance even more cash in order to make short term improvements and thereafter sell the entire loan position or allow for the borrower to sell itself, often at a loss.

Sophisticated healthcare borrowers in default—and the lawyers they hire—understand full well how few good options a lender might have once a loan goes bad and enters a workout situation. The workout may involve a forbearance, working capital advances, replacement financing, reamortization and/or debt reduction. Workout attempts fail (and succeed) for all types of reasons. If no consensual resolution is reached, the dispute invariably ends up in court, including bankruptcy court.

#### 5.11.2.3    *Bad Publicity and Potential Liability*

Large institutional lenders, particularly commercial banks, have a low tolerance for bad publicity. This is due, in part, to the nature of their business model, which stresses long term relationships and the cross-selling of various products and services to customers. Commercial bankers make their money by slowly gaining greater and greater involvement in a borrower's finances, sometimes over many years, by developing trust. Commercial bankers call this process "becoming the client's wallet". Reputation is, therefore, very important. Moreover, the desire of any individual banker may be to avoid embarrassment or the public perception of having made a mistake.

For these reasons, institutional lenders will avoid being responsible for a negative or embarrassing public relations event, if possible. This may include a willingness to lose money, at least over the short run. This sensitivity comes into play in a commercial banker's dealings with a troubled healthcare borrower, especially a not-for-profit. Being the bank that shuts down a nursing home in the poorer section of town is not good press.

### 5.11.3    Special Healthcare Facility Bankruptcy Issues

The Bankruptcy Reform Act of 2005 (the Bankruptcy Act) recognized that healthcare is an important national industry with unique needs. Even the general provisions of the Bankruptcy Act not tailored to healthcare will affect healthcare businesses just as they will affect other industries. In a nutshell, these general provisions make it more difficult for debtors to extinguish unsecured debt—including healthcare-related debt—in bankruptcy.

One significant amendment under the Bankruptcy Act was the addition of Bankruptcy Code Section 333.[15] Section 333 directs a bankruptcy court to appoint an ombudsman in situations where a healthcare provider is in bankruptcy. The ombudsman is tasked with monitoring the quality of patient care during the bankruptcy proceeding and reporting back to the bankruptcy court. If patient care declines, the ombudsman is to inform the court so that appropriate corrective action may be taken.[16]

The premise underlying Section 333 is that the reorganization of a healthcare provider, including cost-reduction measures, should not come at the expense of patient care. The ombudsman can function as a check on debtors and secured lenders, challenging their actions to the extent they jeopardize patient care. Prior to the enactment of Section 333, patients had no direct advocate in Chapter 11 cases.

Perhaps the most troubling amendment from the perspective of debtors and lenders is the addition of Bankruptcy Code Section 362(b)(28).[17] Section 362(b)(28) permits the federal government to unilaterally terminate a healthcare debtor's participation in federal healthcare programs, such as Medicare, without having to seek relief from the automatic stay imposed under Section 362 of the Bankruptcy Code. This new provision deals the federal government a trump card that will make any reorganization of healthcare debt all the more difficult. The government may now simply end its relationship with a healthcare provider, in essence imposing the death penalty on a provider. Section 362(b)(28) will likely cause secured lenders to further worry about receivables-based collateral once a healthcare borrower falls on hard times. This, in turn, may chill lending to cash-strapped healthcare providers, undermine their liquidity, and thereby make it all the more likely that they file bankruptcy petitions in the first place.

In sum, the Bankruptcy Act's various provisions have a mixed effect on healthcare, with some provisions facilitating private healthcare finance and others hampering it.

### 5.12    Special California Rules

California has enacted laws related to real estate loans that are particularly important to understand in the context of healthcare lending. In particular, the one action and anti-deficiency rules can limit the rights of lenders to recover against a borrower under certain circumstances.

---

[15]  11 U.S.C. § 333.

[16]  *See* 11 U.S.C. § 333(b)(3).

[17]  11 U.S.C. § 362(b)(28).

### 5.12.1    One Action Rule

Section 726(a) of the California Code of Civil Procedure encompasses the one action rule. The one action rule addresses three aspects regarding the enforcement of a real property secured obligation: (a) the security first rule, which prevents a real property secured creditor from ignoring its security and suing on the underlying note or debt;[18] (b) the one action principle, which requires a real property secured creditor to enforce all of its security in a single action;[19] and (c) the one form of action rule, which provides that there is only one form of action by which a real property secured creditor can seek to enforce a debt, and that action is by judicial foreclosure.[20] For example, under the security first rule, if a lender sued a borrower on the promissory note first, the borrower could raise the security first rule as a defense and have the case dismissed, or the borrower could let the case proceed, and after the case was over, the effect of the security first rule would be that lender would have lost its security and could never foreclose on the deed of trust.

Similarly, the one action rule can be violated by an enforcement action that is taken by a lender against a borrower outside of a court proceeding.[21] For example, if a lender exercises its set-off right against a borrower's bank account, that enforcement action would violate the security first and one action rule. Since healthcare facilities are operating entities, these rules can be a trap for the unwary. A lender may want to get control of the cash quickly, but in doing so, it may preclude other remedies.[22] Accordingly, lenders need to be aware that they must enforce all of its security in one action.[23]

### 5.12.2    No Deficiency Judgment After Non-Judicial Foreclosure

If a lender pursues a non-judicial foreclosure, and the property is sold, and there is a deficiency, the anti-deficiency rules prohibit the lender from suing the borrower for the deficiency.[24] The price for pursuing non-judicial foreclosure is that the lender gives up the ability to recover any deficiency from the borrower after the non-judicial foreclosure. However, a non-judicial foreclosure has certain advantages over a judicial foreclosure. For example, a non-judicial foreclosure is generally a less expensive and quicker process.

---

[18]  *See Walker v. Community Bank*, 10 Cal 3d 729, 733-34 (1974).

[19]  Cal. Civ. Proc. Code § 726(a). The "action" is generally defined as a judicial proceeding prosecuted to judgment or the judicial or non-judicial appropriation of the debtor's non-collateral assets, such as prejudgment attachment on a bank account. However, neither non-judicial foreclosure nor the mere commencement of judicial foreclosure are considered an "action" within the meaning of Cal. Civ. Proc. Code §§ 22 or 726(a), since neither has been reduced to a judgment.

[20]  *Id.*

[21]  Common violations of the one action rule occur when a creditor (i) proceeds directly on the note before foreclosing on the security and obtains a judgment; (ii) fails to include all of the security in a judicial foreclosure action and following a judgment attempts to enforce the remainder of the security; or (iii) exercises self-help remedies after a debtor's default (*e.g.*, set-off against a bank account, exercise of banker's lien or appropriation of unpledged assets). However, note that under Cal. Civ. Code § 2938(c)(4) and (e)(2), neither the exercise of a creditor's rights under § 2938 of the California Civil Code (*e.g.*, appointment of a receiver and collection and application of rents), nor the presentment, receipt of payment, or demand for payment under a letter of credit constitute an action for purposes of the one action rule (Cal. Civ. Proc. Code § 580.5).

[22]  Cal. Civ. Code § 2938 allows the appointment of a receiver and collection and application of rents as well as demand for payment under a letter of credit.

[23]  *See* Cal. Com. Code § 9604(a) for the foreclosure of personal property and creditors' remedies in connection with mixed collateral foreclosure. Other exceptions to the one action rule include Cal. Com. Code § 726.5 addressing environmentally impaired real property, Cal. Com. Code § 891(g) addressing misappropriation of rents, and certain rights of sold-out junior creditors (*see Roseleaf Corp. v. Chierighino*, 59 Cal. 2d 35, 39 (1963)).

[24]  *See* Cal. Civ. Proc. Code § 580(d).

### 5.12.3    Deficiency Judgment After Judicial Foreclosure

If a lender files a judicial foreclosure, and the property is sold, and there is a deficiency, then subject to the anti-deficiency rules, by following certain required procedures, the lender can obtain a judgment in the foreclosure case against the borrower for the deficiency.[25]

### 5.12.4    Fair Value Limit on Deficiency Judgment

The anti-deficiency rule also places a limit on the amount of the deficiency judgment that can be obtained by a lender after a judicial foreclosure sale.[26] Following the sale, the court will determine the fair value of the property at the time of the sale. If the fair value is greater than the foreclosure sale proceeds, the deficiency judgment will be limited to the difference between the unpaid loan amount and the fair value amount. The result will be that the lender does not recover the full amount of the deficiency.

### 5.12.5    Guarantor Liability

If a loan is guaranteed, the lender must consider the effect of the special California rules discussed above on the guaranty. As a general matter, a guarantor probably will not be liable to a lender if, based on these rules, the borrower is not liable. Thus, a guarantor may not be liable for a deficiency after a non-judicial foreclosure, regardless of the type of loan or property, but may be liable for a deficiency after a judicial foreclosure, subject to the fair market value limitation discussed above.[27]

Guaranties are often written to include a waiver by the guarantor of suretyship defenses, including a lender's election of remedies, one action protections, and the anti-deficiency provisions. It is not clear whether such a waiver is enforceable under California law, and the trend of court decisions does not bode well for a lender's ability to enforce a waiver.[28] Thus, even if a lender holds a guaranty that contains a waiver, the lender may need to pursue judicial foreclosure in order to be certain that it will be able to recover any deficiency against the guarantor.

The result of these California-specific provisions is that lenders must exercise special care in structuring real-estate based loans in California. These rules can also affect portfolio transactions, where a lender is making a loan to multiple properties and one or more of the properties is located in California. Similarly, since loans to healthcare facilities often involve both term loans secured by real estate and working capital revolving loans, it is imperative to structure these loans carefully.

---

[25]  Cal. Civ. Proc. Code § 580(b). If the creditor is entitled to a deficiency judgment, the creditor must apply for the deficiency amount within three months following the foreclosure sale. *See* Cal. Civ. Proc. Code § 726(b).

[26]  *See* Cal. Civ. Proc. Code § 726(b).

[27]  *See Bank of Southern California v. Dombrow* (ordered not published March 14, 1996; former opinion at 39 Cal. App. 4th 1457 (1995)).

[28]  *See id.* and *Cathay Bank v. Lee*, 14 Cal. App. 4th 1533 (1993). *See also* the model waivers set forth in Cal. Civ. Code § 2856.

# 6

# Four Prototypical Deals and Their Related Documents

## 6.1    Type 1—Cash Flow Loans

### 6.1.1    Specific Credit Agreement Provisions

Loan agreements for cash flow loans focus primarily on providing the lender with assurances regarding the borrower's credit profile and generating performance. Since the loan is made on the basis of the cash generated by the business, the lender does not generally rely upon, or require, extensive representations, warranties or covenants regarding the borrower's other assets. The loan agreement will usually also contain provisions limiting the borrower's ability to incur other debt or material liabilities as a means to protect the borrower's cash and the lender's ability to repay the loan. A cash flow loan often does not include a pledge of assets, other than cash.

### 6.1.2    Financial Covenants

Typical financial covenants for cash flow loans are net worth, minimum EBITDA, fixed charge coverage, and debt service coverage ratio. With limited collateral, lenders rely heavily on financial covenants in cash flow loans as a means to test the borrower's present and future ability to repay the loan.

Cash flow lenders rely upon a borrower's cash flow, often expressed by EBITDA, as a test of whether the company can repay debt. In a highly leveraged transaction, lenders will typically test total debt service as a ratio to EBITDA to evaluate the borrower's ability to comfortably pay the loan. Many highly leveraged buyouts are financed on the premise that, following the acquisition, the company will generate sufficient cash to repay the loan needed to make the acquisition in the first place. Cash flow financing can be difficult for industries that are cyclical in nature or more subject to the effects of a recession. Once healthcare entities can generate relatively smooth and robust cash flows, they become good candidates for cash flow loans.

## 6.2     Type 2—Real Estate Based Loans

### 6.2.1     *Structure*

Many real estate based healthcare facilities are structured with one entity owning the real property and an operating tenant (which may be related or unrelated to the property owner) leasing the property. The operating tenant typically leases the property for a monthly lease payment (which often is a set dollar amount or a percentage of the net revenue of the property) and is solely responsible for operating the property, including generating all cash and accounts receivables. Often, if the operating tenant is related to the property owner, the operating lease will sweep as much cash as possible to the landlord so that the operator will be relatively under-capitalized and the property will therefore be shielded from potential tort claims against the operator. Many lenders have adapted some of the capital markets requirements to this structure, imposing single purpose, or bankruptcy remote, type requirements. For example, a lender will require that the borrower adopt and maintain a purpose limited to owning and operating the healthcare facility and no other unrelated asset. Similarly, the lender will typically impose certain limitations on transactions with affiliates and requirements for borrowers to observe corporate formalities, maintain sufficient reserves, and not commingle funds.

### 6.2.2     Specific Credit Agreement Provisions

One misconception about real estate based loans is that the credit agreement will be different than a credit agreement for any other type of secured loan. As a practical matter, however, the only difference between a real estate based loan and any other secured loan is the nature of the collateral. As a result, the provisions in a credit agreement that are unique to a real estate loans generally relate specifically to the real estate, such as (a) representations, warranties, and covenants regarding title to the property and the use, maintenance, and operation of the property; (b) leasing requirements and covenants; (c) escrows for capital improvements, real estate taxes, and insurance; (d) representations, covenants, and indemnities relating to the environmental condition of the property; and (e) casualty and condemnation provisions.

### 6.2.3     Mortgage and Assignment of Rents

The mortgage is the security instrument that creates a lien on the real property. Some lenders use the mortgage as the primary transaction document, so it includes all of the provisions that might be contained in a loan agreement. The general trend, however, has been to put most of the transaction details into the loan agreement and reduce the mortgage to its basic elements, which are (a) creation of the security interest; (b) the borrower's warranties and obligations regarding title to the property; and (c) lender's remedies. Depending on the state, the mortgage may include an assignment of leases and rents or the assignment of leases and rents will be a separate document. While the mortgage creates an interest in the underlying property, the assignment of leases and rents creates a specific interest in those contracts. As a result, if the lender takes possession of the property, the lender also will be able to require the tenants to perform their obligations under the leases on its behalf.

### 6.2.4    Collateral Assignment of Management Agreement

Lenders often require that a borrower assign its management agreement to the lender as collateral and that the manager subordinate its fees to the loan. After an event of default occurs, the collateral assignment allows the lender, at its option, to assume the borrower's rights and obligations under the management agreement, thereby ensuring continuity in the operations at the property. The subordination of the management fees ensures that amounts payable to the lender will be paid before any amounts payable to the manager in the event that there are not sufficient funds to pay both. In addition, the subordination will ensure that the manager will not be able to record a lien against the property that could prime the mortgage. Finally, the collateral assignment of the management agreement will create a direct relationship between the lender and the manager in which the manager agrees that it will abide by certain of the lender's operational requirements and that the lender may terminate the manager under certain conditions without payment of any termination fees.

### 6.2.5    Environmental Indemnity

If a lender takes a mortgage as security for a loan, the lender will usually require an indemnification from the borrower (and often a guarantor) against any losses that may arise from the environmental condition of the property. Borrowers often struggle with the fact that they are indemnifying the lender from all losses related to the environmental condition of the property whether or not those losses are the fault of the borrower. The environmental indemnity, however, represents an allocation of risk. Unless the documents specify otherwise, lenders are making an assumption that the property does not have any adverse environmental conditions, and they do not want to be affected by any such conditions. On the other hand, by purchasing the property, the borrower already has assumed the environmental risks of the property and, as a result, giving an environmental indemnity to a lender does not necessarily expand a borrower's exposure to potential losses arising from the environmental condition of the property.

### 6.2.6    Non-Recourse Carve-Out Guaranty

In some cases, a lender will agree that a loan will be non-recourse to the borrower or any guarantor and that the lender's only recourse is against the property. This is attractive to borrowers because they are able to compartmentalize their liability and the lender cannot bring any deficiency claims against the borrower or any guarantor. A lender may be willing to make a non-recourse loan so long as it believes that the value of the collateral is adequate security for the debt. There will, however, be certain matters for which lenders require the borrower to have recourse liability. Those matters generally relate to the borrower's dishonesty (*e.g.*, fraud, misrepresentation, misappropriation), environmental liabilities, and willful breach of certain important restrictions in the loan documents (*e.g.*, filing for voluntary bankruptcy). Since many real estate borrowers only have one asset—the real estate—lenders often require that these recourse carve-outs be guaranteed by an entity with assets or a "warm-body" guarantor. This way, there is an additional incentive for the borrower to abide by the loan documents and the lender can have some recourse if the borrower behaves badly.

### 6.2.7 Title Insurance

At the outset of any loan transaction, the borrower will provide a title commitment and a survey of the real property that will be security for the loan. A title commitment is based upon a search of the local records and should identify the owner of the property, indicate whether real estate taxes have been paid, and show all liens and encumbrances that have been recorded against the property. The survey, on the other hand, is a picture of the property, showing the boundaries of the property, any buildings and improvements thereon, and the boundaries of any easements or restrictions that were included in the title commitment. Title and survey are critical pieces of due diligence because they ensure that the lender is obtaining the collateral for which it bargained.

In addition to the value of title and survey as due diligence, title insurance is a critical risk management tool. Upon the closing of the loan, the lender will obtain a title insurance policy (which is based on the title commitment) that insures that the mortgage is a valid lien on the title to the property and that the property is subject only to those liens and encumbrances that are shown on the title insurance policy.

### 6.2.8 What Foreclosure Is and How It Differs from State to State

The process by which a lender enforces its lien against real property is customarily referred to as foreclosure. There are, however, a number of different types of foreclosure. For example, all states permit some sort of judicial foreclosure, pursuant to which the lender institutes a foreclosure action in court and obtains a judgment against the property. Judicial foreclosure is often a lengthy process and can take months or even years, so many states have abbreviated forms of foreclosure, such as powers of sale and non-judicial foreclosures. Overall, foreclosure is a uniquely local matter and is generally governed by statute. As a result, the lender will want to be aware of the remedies that are available in each state in which it is doing business.

### 6.2.9 Fixture Filings

Fixtures refer to goods that are so integrated into real property that an interest in such fixtures arises under real property law. Accordingly, in a real estate financing, a lender will make a fixture filing, which is a financing statement covering goods that constitute fixtures and is filed in the land records. In many cases, the fixture filing may be incorporated into the mortgage so long as the mortgage contains the information necessary to satisfy the UCC requirements.

### 6.2.10 Subordinations and Non-Disturbance Agreements

If a mortgaged property is subject to any leases, then the lender will usually want to establish a direct relationship with the tenant(s) to ensure that it will receive the benefit of its bargain. The reason is that if a lease is in place prior to a mortgage, absent any subordination language in the lease or any agreement between the lender and the tenant, the interest of the tenant in the real property will be senior to that of the lender. If the lease is senior to the mortgage, none of the requirements in the mortgage will be binding upon the tenant and, upon foreclosure, the lender will be subject to the terms of the lease.

The lender will often want to seek a subordination and attornment agreement from each tenant, which means that each tenant agrees that its lease is subordinate to the mortgage and if the lender takes ownership of the property, the tenant will treat the lender as its landlord. Upon foreclosure, the lender will have a choice of whether to terminate the lease or accept the lease and require the tenant to perform its obligations thereunder.

As a practical matter, however, usually only a tenant that is related to the mortgage borrower will sign a subordination and attornment agreement. Most third party tenants will insist upon including a non-disturbance provision pursuant to which the lender agrees that, so long as the tenant is not in default under the lease, the lender will not disturb the tenant's possession of the real property. The non-disturbance provision seemingly undercuts the value of subordinating the lease to the mortgage in the first place, but most subordination, non-disturbance, and attornment agreements contain certain lender-friendly provisions that, for example, ensure that the lender will not be liable for any defaults of the borrower (and prior landlord) under the lease nor will the lender be bound by any amendments to the lease to which it had not consented.

## 6.3    Type 3—Asset Based Loans

### 6.3.1    Credit Agreement

When lenders make asset based loans, they usually care only about the value of its collateral, liquidity, and ability of the borrower to make debt payments. Since the loan is underwritten on the basis of the borrower's assets, the loan agreement will typically contain representations, warranties, covenants and reporting requirements related to the amount, quality and liquidity of the borrower's accounts receivable, inventory, and fixed assets. For asset based loans to pharmaceutical or medical device companies, the value of those companies' intellectual property (*e.g.*, patents and FDA approvals) will serve as a significant part of the company's assets. The borrower may have relatively few financial covenants, but will have certain financial reporting requirements regarding its assets, such as aging of accounts receivable and inventory lists. The lender may require the borrower to enter into a deposit account control agreement or lockbox so that the lender has control over the borrower's cash. For a revolving loan, the lender may collect the borrower's cash and applies it toward repayment of the loan. As the borrower needs additional cash, it draws down on the revolving loan. The lender will usually impose periodic field audits on the borrower to validate the accuracy of collateral reports. Due to the highly related nature of the healthcare industry, lenders need to understand healthcare receivables and inventory in order to assess any revolving loan. To properly underwrite an asset based loan, the lender will want to understand both the healthcare entity's business as well as the industry.

### 6.3.2    Revolving Loan Concept

Often, asset based loans contain a revolving loan component, pursuant to which the borrower's current assets serve as a borrowing base for the loan. A revolving loan can assist a healthcare entity with significant accounts receivable and/or inventory to utilize those current assets as collateral to obtain cash prior to such accounts receivable being paid or inventory sold. The lender often imposes restrictions upon what accounts receivable or inventory would be considered eligible for inclusion in the borrowing base. For example, accounts receivable older than 90 days are often excluded as well as some receivables from certain types of payors. For healthcare entities, lenders closely evaluate payor mix. A lender may impose sublimits or restrictions in the event the healthcare entity's receivables are too dependent upon a single payor. Also, a lender may exclude private pay receivables, DSH payments, or capitation payments. Similarly, inventory that constitutes work-in-process, slow moving, or obsolete inventory is usually excluded. A borrowing base is often calculated at 70 to 85% of accounts receivable and 50 to 70% of inventory. The borrower is required to make interest payments only and the revolving loan balance increases and decreases based upon the borrower's assets and draws on the loan. Asset-based term loans, on the other hand, are underwritten based upon the value of the borrower's fixed assets.

### 6.3.3    Financial Covenants

Lenders will usually test and monitor financial covenants, such as debt service coverage ratio and net worth.

### 6.3.4    Sublimits for Standby Letters of Credit

Many asset based loans are made in combination with other financial products such as letters of credit. Borrowers often need to post letters of credit with respect to their business operations in order to obtain goods and services from third parties on credit. A lender providing a revolving loan will often create a sublimit of the revolving loan for the issuance of letters of credit.

### 6.3.5    Borrowing Base Certificate

Lenders will usually require the borrower to submit regular borrowing base certificates, demonstrating the value of the collateral relative to the loan. The frequency of the submission of borrowing base certificates will depend upon the borrower's credit risk. Any loss in the value of collateral may trigger a mandatory payment event in order to bring the loan back into the correct ratio with the collateral.

## 6.4    Type 4—Equity Deals

Healthcare providers often look for new ventures in order to diversify and improve their income stream. Similarly, many healthcare providers and companies look for exit strategies for their businesses. To capitalize on these types of opportunities, an injection of permanent equity may be the most appropriate means to realize these goals.

### 6.4.1    Venture Capital

Venture capital generally refers to equity financing in the early-stages of relatively small, rapidly growing companies. Venture capitalists can also provide several rounds of additional funding to companies that have already demonstrated the viability of their businesses but are not seasoned enough to gain access to the public stock market or credit-oriented lending institutions. Venture capital spending for healthcare-related products and services was at a record high in 2007, both in terms of dollars invested ($9.5 billion) and as a share of total venture capital spending (32%).[1] Venture capital often is a riskier endeavor than other forms of equity investment. As a result, any venture capital equity investment typically has the following characteristics:

- The investor has an active, ongoing involvement with the management of the company in which it has invested. From the formulation of business plans to the installation of control procedures, a venture capital firm becomes an integral partner in the activities of its portfolio companies. This activist approach can be beneficial to the healthcare company to the extent that the venture capital partner can provide a broad spectrum of industry knowledge and business discipline to the table.

- The investment horizon is relatively longer than that of a more traditional equity investor within which to realize significant returns. This means that venture capital firms will only make commitments to enterprises with exceptional business promise commensurate with the risk the venture capital firm is taking by investing. Targeted annual rates of return for institutional venture capital firms can range from 35% to more than 115%. Thus, the willingness of a venture capital firm to invest often signals the potential for success of the enterprise.

### 6.4.2    Private Equity

Private equity generally refers to equity investment in more stable, developed companies by private investors. Private equity investors often partner with seasoned healthcare managers or consultants with respect to the operations of their investments. Private equity investors generally realize a return on their equity investment through an initial public offering of the company, sale of the company or other recapitalization of the company. Often, the private equity investor does not realize any cash return until the occurrence of one of these events. As equity, investors only get paid after senior or any junior lenders are paid and their investment is generally unsecured. As a result, private equity investors have the riskiest capital and demand higher returns and greater control over the company. Due to the regulatory nature of healthcare, private equity investors that invest in healthcare entities generally specialize in the healthcare industry. Given issues related to change of ownership, licensure, and reimbursement, such specialization is critical to understanding the investment.

### 6.4.3    Form of Ownership

Because investors have different risk tolerances and return and liquidity objectives, a sophisticated equity investor will utilize a mixture of the various securities discussed below.

#### 6.4.3.1    Common Stock

Common stock (or equivalents, such as warrants) is the most frequently used instrument for purchasing an ownership interest in a company. Common Stock includes the right to vote on certain corporate decisions, which is important for equity owners. In liquidation, however, common stockholders are the last to share in the assets of the corporation, coming after preferred stock owners.

---

[1]  PricewaterhouseCoopers, National Venture Capital Association: MoneyTree Report.

If the company is successful, its shares can be sold through a registered public offering. Stock may be sold without registration under Rule 144 of the Securities Act of 1933. Rule 144 states that non-affiliated purchasers of privately issued common stock (*e.g.*, not registered with the Securities and Exchange Commission) must hold such stock at least one year before selling. In an attempt to avoid Rule 144 constraints, investors generally will insist that registration rights accompany the common stock purchased in an equity financing.

### 6.4.3.2    Preferred or Convertible Preferred Stock

Preferred stock provides an investor with rights that the common shareholder does not have. Preferred stock owners may impose covenants and financial tests that, if not met, provide for control of the board of directors to shift to the preferred investors. Also, many preferred stock agreements possess scheduled mandatory dividend or redemption features, which provide an investment return even if conversion to common stock or a liquidity event does not take place.

### 6.4.3.3    Subordinated or Convertible Debt

Subordinated or convertible debt is used in equity financing situations in which the investor wants the security and yield of a debt instrument. Debt gives an equity investor more options than a straight equity position does. If the company defaults on the loan, the investor can accelerate repayment, and if the company cannot reply, the equity investor (now a creditor) has strong leverage to influence management decisions.

### 6.4.3.4    Limited Liability Companies

Limited liability companies (LLCs) are common investment vehicles especially in the context of real estate investments. LLCs provide pass-through tax treatment while allowing the flexibility to provide for different classes of interests, voting versus non-voting units, preferred returns, specific internal rates of return, and detailed rights of the members and managers.

## 6.4.4    Debt Versus Equity

The line between debt and equity can be blurred. The parties may consider an investment as *equity*, but for tax and accounting purposes that same investment may instead be considered *debt*. For example, equity may have certain dividend payment schedules and required redemption features, similar to debt. Similarly, a lender may loan an entity funds with a debt instrument that has features of both debt and equity. For example, the borrower may have certain contingent payments, the lender may receive a share of the borrower's profits, and the lender may have significant economic risk that all payments may not be made. A lender will carefully structure debt to avoid any claim of equitable subordination since a bankruptcy court has the power to reorder the priority of claims or interests by recharacterizing debt as equity. The analysis of whether an instrument is debt or equity for tax purposes is different than the analysis under financial reporting purposes. As a general matter, debt requires a promise to pay a fixed sum by a certain date, with a reasonable expectation of repayment. The IRS has issued a draft checklist distinguishing debt from equity pursuant to Section 385 of the Internal Revenue Code, but no final regulations have been promulgated. Not only does the characterization of an obligation as debt versus equity have implication in terms of repayment priority, but such characterization may have implications as to whether the company (or borrower) can deduct interest payments. Similarly, a holder of an equity instrument will receive different tax treatment depending upon whether an instrument is characterized as equity or debt. The current tax rate on dividends may provide some incentive for an investor to receive preferred equity. Similarly, if a company has losses, an investor may desire to receive preferred equity and take advantage of a pass-through treatment of losses.

# 7

# Potential Credit Enhancement and Risk Reduction Sources

Credit enhancement devices, as the name suggests, help bolster the safety level of a transaction to a lender or investor. Even where credit risk is absolutely unavoidable in the underlying transaction, a credit enhancement device can lessen risk. The added safety allows a lender to charge a lower rate or perhaps even make a loan that would have been otherwise too risky to make. Credit enhancement is especially important to an industry like healthcare which has traditionally been perceived as high in risk. Credit enhancement not only provides greater financial safety but also can legally simplify a transaction. Resorting to credit enhancement devices can save a lender the complicated, risky, and time-consuming job of liquidation and foreclosure on active healthcare assets pledged as collateral.

## 7.1    Letters of Credit

A letter of credit (LOC) is a three-way contract among a borrower, a financial institution (*i.e.*, a bank or issuer) and a beneficiary/creditor. Under the arrangement, a bank legally obligates itself to pay a certain amount of money to the beneficiary on behalf of the borrower in the event the beneficiary demands payment. A beneficiary/creditor usually only makes a demand for payment on the bank if it feels that borrower will not be able to pay directly and if certain conditions are met. If demand is actually made on the bank for payment, then the amount paid by the bank to the beneficiary becomes a loan from the bank to the borrower.

Under an LOC arrangement, the third party beneficiary/creditor is given certain enforcement conditions and papers which, if presented to the bank's letter of credit department, legally obligate the bank or issuer to pay. The automatic and absolute right to receive payment upon demand distinguishes a LOC from a guaranty, which is a mere contract that a guarantor might breach or may not have funds to honor. The legal right to receive payment is absolute with LOCs. The bank will be obligated to pay if the enumerated funding conditions are legally satisfied by the party demanding payment. A borrower may have a claim to bring against a beneficiary that wrongfully enforces a LOC, but the borrower will have no claim against a bank for making proper payment if the conditions for paying are satisfied.

A hospital may, for example, wish to purchase on credit a large piece of x-ray equipment from a German engineering firm. The hospital has no established reputation and the German firm is worried about delivering the machine and then not getting paid. If a borrower were to arrange for a reputable bank with deep pockets to give the German firm a letter of credit, then the firm would be certain of receiving payment. Such a bank may already have a relationship with the hospital, and may have already conducted due diligence that the German firm was not able to do. With LOC in hand, the firm can then ship the machine immediately, and if the borrower pays them directly, the letter of credit may never be exercised. The bank receives a fee for its services and interest for money lent.

Some letters of credit are even intentionally designed to be drawn down upon, and all three parties so agree in advance. In that instance, LOCs are really nothing more than a way of effecting payment to a third party through a bank.

## 7.2    Insurance

Lenders may accept a variety of types of insurance policies that generally protect against the risk that a borrower will fail to repay a loan. If a borrower defaults, the insurer will—at least theoretically—make the lender whole for its losses. Depending on the transaction, a lender may require a borrower to purchase such a policy in favor of the lender as a condition for making the loan. The insurer will then usually require subrogation rights allowing it pursue its own collection action against the borrower if it ever has to pay under the policy. In essence, an insurer who has to pay out is allowed to step into the lender's shoes as a new creditor to the insured party. If A pays B's debts to C, then A is allowed to collect against B, just as C might have. A is thus subrogated to C. Insurers may also require security interests to secure their contingent exposure.

Savvy lenders accepting insurance policies as security should pay special attention to the wording of the conditions set forth in the policy for payment. Insurance companies will often refuse payment based on a technical distinction between the facts surrounding a payment default and the written conditions for payment found in a policy. For example, a policy that insures against "payment default arising from borrower bankruptcy, reorganization or insolvency" might not cover a loss where a debt is voluntarily reorganized and written down by a lender but where no Chapter 11 bankruptcy filing was actually made.

## 7.3    Guaranties

A guaranty is a contractual promise made to a creditor to pay another person's debt if that person cannot pay such debt by himself. A creditor receiving a guaranty therefore doubles the number of persons against whom it can collect. The wealthier and more trustworthy the guarantor, the more safety the creditor receives.

### 7.3.1    Legal and Structural Issues

A corporation is a separate legal person that incurs its own debts. Those debts are normally not the liabilities of corporate shareholders and officers, which is the one of the major reasons corporations exist. The *doctrine of limited liability* shields shareholders from having to pay corporate debt. At times, however, the only way for a corporation with limited assets to obtain financing is for shareholders with deep pockets to guaranty corporate debt. In other words, shareholders with significant assets are asked to give up their limited liability protections in order to facilitate the financing of their corporate business ventures. Similarly, lenders will often also seek guaranties from a corporation's affiliates and subsidiaries in order to obtain recourse to their assets as well.

Some such guaranties created among members of a corporate family may be of limited use, however, because they may effect a fraudulent conveyance. A fraudulent conveyance occurs, in a nutshell, when a corporation either intentionally or unintentionally enters into a transaction in which it gives more in value than it receives, and the resulting loss of wealth makes it impossible to pay existing creditors.

When a parent corporation guaranties a loan made to a subsidiary, it is called a *down stream* guaranty. The parent benefits from the loan made to the subsidiary because the parent owns stock in the subsidiary. Consequently, the parent receives something of equivalent value for the guaranty it gives. The same is not the case, however, when a subsidiary guaranties the debts of its parent in an *up stream* guaranty. The subsidiary has now incurred a contingent liability and has nothing to show for it in return because the subsidiary does not own stock in the parent. If the guaranty or its enforcement causes the subsidiary to become insolvent, its preexisting creditors may attempt to nullify the guaranty by alleging a fraudulent conveyance. The question will then become whether the loan to the parent benefited the subsidiary, which may or may not be the case.

Careful bankers and lawyers will therefore take care to study the relationships between corporations before placing great reliance on certain types of guaranties. Similarly, a lender's counsel has to be careful with existing guaranties when a deal is amended or renegotiated. Often, guarantor consent to the changes must be obtained, especially where they potentially increase the term or the liability arising under the guaranty. Such changes, if not consented to by guarantor, may not bind guarantor with respect to increased liability, and may in some jurisdictions completely abrogate the guaranty.

### 7.3.2    Variations in Guaranty Form and Structure

Guaranties can come in many forms. Their adaptability makes them a useful tool in many financings. Some of the more commonly seen variations are as follows:

#### 7.3.2.1    *Limited Guaranties*

A limited guaranty provides that guarantor puts a maximum dollar limit on how much it will pay.

#### 7.3.2.2    *Secured Guaranties*

In a secured guaranty, the guarantor puts up collateral to back his, her, or its obligations under the guaranty.

### 7.3.2.3    Non-Recourse Guaranties

As discussed above, a non-recourse loan provides the creditor a limited pool of assets against which it has recourse to collect. A non-recourse guaranty provides certain carve-outs to the non-recourse nature of a loan, and allows the lender to expand its ability to collect on the loan.

### 7.3.2.4    Guaranties of Payment or of Collection

The legal difference between a guaranty of collection and a guaranty of payment constitutes a trap for the unwary creditor. A mere guaranty of *collection* means that a creditor must first exhaust collection remedies against the primary borrower before turning to the guarantor for payment. A guaranty of *payment*, on the other hand, does not require a creditor to take any action against creditor as a prerequisite to enforcement.

## 7.4    Interest Rate Risk Protection for Variable Rate Loans: Derivatives, Swaps, and other Hedging Devices

As discussed above, the interest that a creditor charges is its source of profit and reimbursement for the risks it runs of not getting repaid in full. Interest on a loan can either be fixed at the start of a loan at a particular percent rate, or interest can "float" during the life of a loan. A floating interest rate can be tied to LIBOR,[1] the fed funds rate, a bank's own internal prime rate,[2] or any other objective measure. Such floating rates will rise and fall from period to period depending on how the market place is rewarding risk-taking at any given historical moment. A discussion of the "risk premium" for lending is beyond the scope of this monograph, but suffice it to say that lenders will demand higher interest during unstable economic times when the chances of not getting repaid are higher than normal.

Unless interest is fixed at a particularly high rate—something a borrower may object to—a fixed rate exposes a creditor to particularly risk that times will change. A price fixed years ago during good times might not adequately compensate a lender years later when risk premiums are higher because of recession, international crisis, or similar events. Real-estate based loans, where the collateral is primarily one or more parcels of land, with fixed income streams, often lend themselves more readily to a fixed rate. A floating rate provides a creditor with protection because it allows reward to adjust to risk. Unfortunately, a floating rate that floats too high during bad times may expose a weaker borrower to potentially higher payments that it will not be able to afford, thus forcing an otherwise healthy loan into default.

To cure this problem, creditors and debtors often enter into floating rate loans backed by hedging devices that ensure that a borrower will always be able to pay interest, even if rates float beyond the borrower's ability to pay them. This gives the creditor the security of a variable rate, without the risk that the variable rate will break the borrower. Hedging devices come in many forms. A swap agreement, for example, is a contract in which the borrower effectively trades away the risk that interest will climb. The counterparty buying the risk makes money as long as rates stay low but must

---

[1]  LIBOR is the London Interbank Offered Rate, which is the rate international banks charge each other for loans.
[2]  When a bank or lender offers its prime rate to a borrower the borrower should be aware that the rate offered is not necessarily the lowest rate a bank has on offer, the use of the word "prime" notwithstanding.

pay borrower's variable rate when it climbs above a certain amount. Thus, once rates float above a certain level, the borrower no longer pays but the lender still gets paid. Often, the money required to purchase such a swap contract comes straight from loan proceeds at the insistence of the lender. In some structures, the lender is also a swap counterparty. Similarly, many lenders insist upon a collateral assignment of the swap agreement as additional security for the loan. On the other hand, a borrower can enter into a synthetic floating rate swap whereby a borrower converts a fixed rate liability to a floating rate liability.

## 7.5    Cross-Default and Collateralization Provisions

Certain types of credit enhancement do not involve giving creditors access to more sources of repayment but rather to more *legal rights*. From a borrower's point of view, legal rights can be initially cheaper to give away, but the consequences can be drastically more expensive in the end. As discussed above, most credit agreements contain a list of events of default. A cross-default provision provides that any default that occurs in connection with Loan A will also constitute a default under Loan B, even though Loan B might otherwise be in perfectly good health, or vice-versa. Without the cross-default, a borrower might decide to allow certain loans to go into default by not paying them and then use the saved money to keep other loans in good stead. Thus, a borrower who agrees to give a lender a cross-default is agreeing that it will potentially lose all of its loan facilities if even one of them goes bad.

A cross-default right is enhanced by a cross-collateralization right. Assume a situation in which Loan A is secured by a mortgage on a hospital building, and Loan B is secured by receivables. Under a cross-default, if Loan A goes bad, a lender will also be able to call in Loan B, even though B is being properly paid. However, without a cross-collateralization right, a lender would still not be able to liquidate the receivables to pay off Loan A, because such receivables are not part of the collateral securing Loan A. Cross-collateralization allows for a lender to liquidate the collateral securing any of its loans in order to collect on any of its loans. This is important in the event that collateral securing one loan is actually worth more than the loan. The extra collateral "cushion" can then be applied to a different loan, whereas without cross-collateralization it would be the borrower's to keep.

## 7.6    Equity Infusions

Another way to enhance the credit quality of a loan is to increase the amount of equity invested in the borrower. A lender often will only make a loan to a company if a company's owners first buy additional stock in that company, for cash.

## 7.7    Subordinated and Mezzanine Debt

As described above, the existence of mezzanine debt provides credit enhancement to more senior types of debt, which see mezzanine creditors as an extra layer protecting them from losses. Thus, the existence of mezzanine debt may make it easier for a borrower to also obtain more senior credit. Similarly, subordinated debt (or second lien loans) can provide another layer of debt and add to credit enhancement from the perspective of a senior lender. With various layers of debt, lenders will negotiate various intercreditor and subordination agreements to document the relative "pecking order" controlling each creditor's rights and obligations.

## 7.8      Syndication

A lender is often able to make a loan of a particular size or type based upon its own credit policies, with the assumption that the lender will hold the loan on its own books. In order to facilitate larger or potentially "riskier" loans, lenders often look to syndicate a loan as a means to spread risk. So, while a borrower generally does not syndicate its own loan as a means to spread risk and enhance the credit, a borrower may instead work with an agent, arranger, or bookrunner that will arrange for various lenders to make the entire loan amount. As a benchmark, at the time of publication, a single lender is generally reluctant or unable to make a loan in excess of $50 million when the lender is intending to hold that loan on its own books or balance sheet. Loan transactions in excess of $50 million generally will be syndicated. Accordingly, either an agent arranges for multiple lenders to make loans at the time of closing the loan, or a single lender makes the entire loan and then sells pieces of the existing loan to other lenders or investors in a secondary market.

Increasingly, lenders will require a syndication contingency in any term sheet or commitment that reflects the then-current secondary market. Recently, many lenders found themselves having to discount loans when selling them on the secondary market. Accordingly, lenders and agents are trying to push that risk onto the borrowers. The last thing a lender wants to do is promise to make a loan at a below-market price, and then fail to attract other lenders to the transaction. Such a lender will then be forced to take the entire position onto its own book at a risk-to-reward ratio that is obviously no longer "market." Lenders are therefore including flex language that gives the lender the ability to increase pricing to a certain level in order to syndicate the loan to the market. While borrowers would prefer a firm commitment, forcing a lender to guess what future market pricing might invite the lender to walk away.

## 7.9      Capital Markets & Securitization

### 7.9.1      Overview

Broken down to its most essential, all finance and investing is a question of matchmaking. Capital cannot grow unless it is harnessed to a "going concern"—in other words, a business operation which incurs risks and creates value. Money kept in a shoebox loses value. Conversely, businesses cannot exist without access to and use of capital. Perhaps the most traditional way in which capital is wed to a going concern is a straightforward loan by a bank to a business.

Capital can also be accessed, however, through the capital markets through a process of securitization. Instead of making a promise to repay a loan using future revenues, a business effectively packages its future revenues inside a security. The security is then sold in the capital markets just like any other stock or bond, depending on its characteristics. The parties buying the securities do not own equity in the issuer but rather own a certain bundle of legal rights to receive future payments that would have otherwise gone to the issuer.

Securitization can be a very important tool because it allows those with specialized lending expertise to make far more loans than they normally would if they only had their own money to lend. A bank with expertise in lending to a particular type of company, such as a hospital, can make various loans to hospitals and then immediately sell these loans to potentially thousands of investors by repackaging the loans as securities. With the proceeds of the sale, the lender can then make additional loans rather than having to wait for the first loan to be repaid. Because the loans can be securitized in any number of smaller allotments and the securities themselves given any number of characteristics, the total pool of capital available to borrowers increases and therefore the cost of borrowing decreases.

Instead of looking to perhaps a half dozen regional banks as the finite set of potential sources of capital, securitization allows a healthcare provider in need of cash to obtain capital from any investor in the world with access to the capital markets.

### 7.9.2     Difficulty of Securitizing Healthcare Mortgages or Assets

In a commercial mortgage-based securities (CMBS) transaction, various mortgage loans are pooled and transferred to a trust. The trust then issues a series of bonds or notes. Nationally recognized rating agencies such as Standard & Poor's or Moody's Investor Service then assign credit ratings to the bond or note classes.

Relatively few healthcare mortgage loans have been included in CMBS transactions. Healthcare mortgage loans that lend themselves to CMBS-type transactions are typically mortgage loans made solely to real estate investors that have leased their facilities to unaffiliated healthcare operators. Since CMBS loans are generally highly standardized, healthcare loans that require specialized loan covenants and incorporate regulatory provisions do not easily lend themselves to CMBS transactions. The Standard & Poor's CMBS Legal and Structured Finance Criteria provides specific approved representations, warranties, and covenants for stand-alone property specific, large senior housing, and long-term care facility loan transactions (*see* **Appendix A**). Since CMBS transactions historically provided for additional liquidity in the market as well as the ability to limit risk, agency lenders were often able to offer CMBS loans at very competitive lower rates. Unfortunately, many healthcare borrowers have traditionally been unable to avail themselves of these opportunities, and their cost of capital therefore has increased accordingly.

Given a high volume of loans to review and secure, CMBS bond buyers generally shy away from loan pools with healthcare loans or healthcare collateral. Such bond buyers generally do not have the time or experience to understand the collateral and underwrite the associated risk. Similarly, at a time when CMBS transactions are considered risky, bond buyers are disinclined to accept healthcare assets. The issue becomes self-perpetuating in that if CMBS bond buyers do not see many performing asset pools containing healthcare loans, even if such loans are well-priced, buyers may see these loans as being too risky and non-standard to include into a pool. Accordingly, lenders will avoid placing such loans into pools out of fear that it would be difficult to sell the pool to bond buyers.

The same basic problems affecting healthcare real estate assets also effect healthcare receivables. Securitization works best when the loan and collateral assets that are being fed into the conversion system cause as little indigestion as possible before they come out the other end as securities. Any receivable, for example, that cannot be easily assigned causes problems which makes the receivable less than ideal for securitization.

### 7.9.3 Special Healthcare Related Issues Raised by Fitch and Moody's

While certain types of healthcare loans may be disfavored in CMBS transactions, Standard & Poor's and other rating agencies rate investment grade (and non-investment grade) non-profit healthcare debt, primarily in relation to bond issuances. The various rating agencies have issued specific, healthcare-related considerations when evaluating debt issued to healthcare borrowers. The existence of transparent rules of evaluation starts the process of making healthcare loans more easily understandable and therefore more capable of being easily securitized in the future.

In June 2005, Moody's Investors Service published "Governance of Not-For-Profit Healthcare Organizations" (the Moody's Report). The Moody's Report outlines various aspects of corporate governance that Moody's will consider when rating debt issued to non-profit healthcare entities. For example, Moody's will review the healthcare entity's board composition and performance, the selection and evaluation of senior management, financial reporting, use of performance metrics, and conflict of interest policies.

On August 9, 2005, Fitch published a Healthcare Special Report entitled, "Sarbanes-Oxley and Not-For-Profit Hospitals" (the Fitch Report). The Fitch Report takes a stronger position than the Moody's Report. The Fitch Report takes the position that the Sarbanes-Oxley Act of 2002 (SOX) requirements, including the requirements related to internal controls over financial reporting, constitute best practices and thus should be adopted by hospitals and healthcare systems. In assessing the creditworthiness of hospitals and healthcare systems, Fitch now will review compliance with SOX. In its rating, Fitch will evaluate items such as: (a) whether the hospital or healthcare system has an audit committee; (b) the composition of the audit committee; (c) the code of conduct or code of ethics policy; (d) the whistleblower policy; (e) the requirement to provide audited financial statements; (f) management certification of financial statements; and (g) the adoption of internal controls.

In anticipation of further regulation, and in recognition of standards of best practices, non-profit healthcare entities have begun to adopt certain aspects of SOX. Similarly, both rating agencies and financial institutions have begun to review corporate governance aspects of non-profit healthcare entities as an essential component of a healthcare entity's credit profile. While many bond issuances and/or debt instruments held by hospitals, health systems, and other healthcare providers are not rated, this development by the rating agencies signals the standardization of lender requirements of healthcare entities with respect to corporate governance and financial reporting. Given the recent enforcement activities of the IRS with respect to excess compensation, investigations by Congress of non-profit institutions, and various state initiatives requiring certain accountability and disclosures by non-profit entities, these corporate governance requirements are becoming standard practice among healthcare entities. Whether or not the debt is rated, healthcare lenders are then likely to impose these standards when underwriting and making loans to healthcare entities.

# 8

# Conclusion

As discussed throughout this monograph, the healthcare industry is capital intensive, dynamic, and highly regulated. Lending to and investing in healthcare entities requires specialized industry knowledge and often complex structuring with respect to underwriting and documenting the transaction.

The efficient markets theory holds that it is not possible to beat the market. Everything already known or knowable about a investment, as well as everything that can be reasonably predicted about an investment or an economic sector, is already discounted into current pricing. However, the efficient market theory may break down when it comes to healthcare. Complex economic, demographic, and technological issues may blunt the effect of the efficient market theory as applied to the healthcare industry.

If the uncertainty and complexity of the healthcare industry frustrates the theory of efficient markets, then it may be possible to beat the market through wisely made and properly structured financings or investments. The growth, risks, and rewards inherent in the healthcare industry may bring the opportunity for greater return. By understanding the healthcare industry and by carefully structuring transactions, savvy lenders and investors will be in a good position to benefit from increasing demand for healthcare capital.

# Appendix A

### S&P Guidelines for Long Term Care Financing[1]

- *Compliance with laws*. Each facility operator or manager, each borrower, and each senior housing, nursing, or skilled nursing facility is in compliance with all applicable federal, state, and local laws, regulations (including any government payment program requirements and disclosure of ownership and related information requirements), quality and safety standards, accepted professional standards, and principles that apply to professionals providing services in such facilities, accreditation standards, and requirements of the applicable state department of health and all other federal, state, or local governmental authorities including, without limitation, those requirements relating to the facility's physical structure and environment, licensing, quality, and adequacy of medical care, distribution of pharmaceuticals, rate setting, equipment, personnel, operating policies, additions to facilities, and services and fee splitting. For as long as the rated securities are outstanding, each facility that is owned, leased, or operated by a borrower or an operator or manager shall be operated in compliance with such laws and requirements.

- *Licenses*. All governmental licenses, permits, regulatory agreements, or other approvals or agreements necessary or desirable for the use and operation of each facility as intended are held by the applicable borrower, operator, or manager in the name of the borrower and are in full force and effect, including, without limitation, approved provider status in any approved provider payment program and a valid certificate of need or similar certificate, license, or approval issued by the applicable state department of health (or any subdivision thereof) or the state licensing agency, as applicable, for the requisite number of beds (collectively, the "licenses"). As long as the rated securities remain outstanding, each borrower shall operate its facility or cause its facility to be operated in a manner such that the licenses shall remain in full force and effect.

- *Ownership of licenses*. The licenses, including without limitation, the certificate of need: may not be, and have not been, transferred to any location other than the facility; have not been pledged as collateral security for any other loan or indebtedness; and are held free from restrictions or known conflicts that would materially impair the use or operation of the facility as intended, and are not provisional, probationary, or restricted in any way.

- *Effectiveness of and amendments to licenses and bed capacity*. So long as the rated securities remain outstanding, no borrower, operator, or manager shall: rescind, withdraw, revoke, amend, modify, supplement, or otherwise alter the nature, tenor, or scope of the licenses, or applicable provider payment program participation, for any facility; amend or otherwise change any facility's authorized bed capacity and/or the number of beds approved by the applicable

---

[1] Standard & Poor's, U.S. CMBS Legal and Structured Finance Criteria, May 1, 2003, pages 37–39.

state department of health or other applicable state licensing agency; or replace or transfer all or any part of any facility's beds to another site or location.

- *Medicare/Medicaid compliance*. Each senior housing facility is in compliance with all requirements for participation in Medicaid, including without limitation, the Medicare and Medicaid Patient and Program Protection Act of 1987, and each nursing or skilled nursing facility is in compliance with all requirements for participation in Medicare and Medicaid. Each facility is in conformance in all material respects with all insurance, reimbursement, and cost reporting requirements, and has a current provider agreement that is in full force and effect under Medicare and Medicaid, as applicable.

- *Third-party payors*. There is no threatened or pending revocation, suspension, termination, probation, restriction, limitation, or nonrenewal affecting any borrower, operator, manager, or facility of any participation or provider agreement with any third-party payor, including Medicare, Medicaid, Blue Cross and/or Blue Shield, and any other private commercial insurance managed care and employee assistance program (such programs, the "Third-Party Payor Programs") to which any borrower, operator or manager presently is subject. All Medicare, Medicaid, and private insurance cost reports and financial reports submitted by each borrower, operator or manager are and will be materially accurate and complete and have not been and will not be misleading in any material respects. No cost reports for any facility remain "open" or unsettled, except as otherwise disclosed.

- *Governmental proceedings and notices*. No borrower, operator, manager, or facility is currently the subject of any proceeding by a governmental agency, and no notice of any violation has been received from a governmental agency that would, directly or indirectly, or with the passage of time, have a material adverse impact on any borrower's ability to accept and/or retain patients or result in the imposition of a fine, a sanction, a lower rate certification, or a lower reimbursement rate for services rendered to eligible patients; modify, limit or annul, or result in the transfer, suspension, revocation, or imposition of probationary use of any borrower's licenses; or affect any borrower's continued participation in Medicare, Medicare, or Third-Party Payor Programs, as applicable, or any successor programs thereto, at current rate certifications.

- *Physical plant standards*. Each facility and the use thereof complies in all material respects with all applicable local, state, and federal building codes, fire codes, healthcare, nursing facility, and other similar regulatory requirements and no waivers of such physical plant standards exist at any of the facilities.

- *Past violations of senior housing facilities*. No senior housing facility has received a statement of charges or deficiencies and no penalty enforcement actions have been undertaken against any such facility, its operator, manager, or borrower, or against any officer, director, or stockholder thereof, by any governmental agency during the last three calendar years, and there have been no violations over the past three years that have threatened any such facility's, operator's, manager's, or borrower's certification for participation in any Third-Party Payor Programs.

- ***Past violations of nursing and skilled nursing facilities***. No nursing or skilled nursing facility has been cited with a "G" level deficiency or higher. No statement of charges or deficiencies has been made and no penalty enforcement action has been undertaken against any such facility, its operator, manager, or borrower, or against any officer, director, or stockholder thereof, by any governmental agency during the last survey cycle. Furthermore, no nursing or skilled nursing facility has been the subject of a "double G" determination for the last three years.

- ***Audits***. There are no current, pending, or outstanding Medicare, Medicaid, or Third-Party Payor Programs reimbursements audits or appeals pending at any of the facilities, and there are no years that are subject to audits.

- ***Recoupment***. There are no current or pending Medicare, Medicaid, or Third-Party Payor Programs recoupment efforts at any of the facilities. None of the borrowers are participants in any federal program whereby any governmental agency may have the right to recover funds by reason of the advance of federal funds, including, without limitation, those authorized under the Hill-Burton Act.

- ***Pledge of receivables***. No borrower has pledged its receivables as collateral security for any other loan or indebtedness.

- ***Patient care agreements***. There are no patient or resident care agreements with patients or residents or with any other persons that deviate in any material adverse respect from the standard form customarily used at the facilities.

- ***Patient records***. All patient or resident records at each facility, including patient or resident trust fund accounts, are true and correct in all material respects.

- ***Management and operating agreements***. Any existing agreement relating to the management or operation of any facility with respect to any facility is in full force and effect and is not in default by any party thereto. In the event any management or operating agreement is terminated or in the event of foreclosure or other acquisition of a facility by the trustee for the benefit of the holders of the rated securities, the applicable borrower, the trustee, any subsequent operator, manager, or any subsequent purchaser need not obtain a certificate of need prior to applying for and receiving a license to operate such facility or prior to receiving Medicare or Medicaid payments, as applicable.

- ***Payment procedures***. No facility, operator, manager, or borrower shall, other than in the normal course of business, change the terms of any of the Third-Party Payor Programs or its normal billing payment or reimbursement policies and procedures with respect thereto, including without limitation the amount and timing of finance charges, fees, and write-offs.

# Appendix B

## A Short Primer on Debt, Equity, and Legal Terminology for Beginners

The world of financial products can be divided into two broad types: debt and equity. Debt is created when a lender makes a loan to a healthcare provider or company that must be paid back, and often must be paid back before the owners of the provider can take distributions or otherwise liquidate the provider. Holders of debt generally get to go to the front of the line when it comes time to be repaid, and because they lower their risk of loss by being in front of the repayment line, they do not generally share in the profits of the business as equity holders. Equity is a direct investment in the provider and an agreement to share the risks and rewards of direct ownership. Because equity holders take more risk of losing their investment, they also profit most when the enterprise does well.

Equity ownership generally means stock ownership. Various financial devices can blur the distinction between debt and equity such as subordinated loans, mezzanine loans, and preferred stock. These concepts roam in the middle ground between debt and equity. For example, at times borrowers will reward a lender for making a loan by granting the lender warrants that allow the lender to purchase stock in a borrower. This way, the lender gets some "up side" in the event the enterprise goes well.

Debt can be divided into two broad classes: secured and unsecured. Unsecured debt, as the name suggests, is debt that is not backed by any sort of collateral or other assets that a lender might sell or take if a borrower cannot repay in cash. Unsecured debt is backed by nothing more than a borrower's promise to repay. It is therefore usually a riskier type of debt, and more interest is often charged for it. Trade creditors usually fall under the category of unsecured creditors. A debt becomes "secured" when assets and property are pledged to the lender such that the lender (and usually only the lender) can use such assets to repay the loan in the event the borrower cannot pay. Secured debt deals become more complicated than non-secured, because the deal documents must cover how collateral interest will be measured, pledged, released, and "perfected".

Because a secured lender has additional protections that an unsecured lender does not, it runs less risk and can charge less. Thus, if a borrower has sufficient unclaimed collateral that could be used to help secure a loan, it can be in a borrower's best economic interest to make a lender as secure as possible. Of course, a dollar's worth of collateral can usually only be pledged once, and once it is pledged, the option to enter into future secured financings is lost. Borrowers may prefer to keep certain assets unencumbered so that they would be able to pledge such assets for another secured loan if needed.

The receipt of a "security interest" in collateral happens in two stages. First, the lender and borrower must enter a contract that "creates" or "attaches" a security interest to particular collateral. The definition of what the collateral will be can become complicated, for instance, when collateral consists of a pool of promised payments from third parties. The second stage in any secured transaction is called "perfection" and takes place when the lender makes a public claim on certain collateral, thereby giving all future lenders and creditors notice that such assets are already hypothecated. Perfection can generally take place with a filing of a "UCC-1 Financing Statement." A UCC-1 Financing Statement must be filed in the borrower's state of formation. Liens on certain types of collateral such as accounts, inventory, equipment, and general intangibles can only be perfected by filing a UCC-1 Financing Statement. Other types of collateral, such as bank accounts, can only be perfected by obtaining control. Accordingly, lenders will require a deposit account control agreement between a borrower's deposit bank and the lender to obtain such control. Still other types of collateral, such as stock, can only be perfected by possession. However, at times lenders will want to take matters a step further than simply staking a claim by actually taking control of the collateral while loans are outstanding. Generally speaking, Article 9 of the Uniform Commercial Code governs secured transactions.

As a final pointer, loan products tend to come in one of two forms. Term loans are simple outlays of cash as a loan, which are then repaid over time as agreed by the parties. The lender loans the borrower money, which is then repaid. Alternatively, revolving loans are loans that function just as credit cards function. Under a revolving loan, a borrower can borrow and repay the lender many times, provided that they do not go over a certain total limit of aggregate indebtedness, and provided further that they completely repay the loan and cease borrowing at the end of the revolving loan's life.

# Appendix C

### Sample Opinion
### Long Term Care Facility
### (Real Estate Loan)

1. Borrower, [**Guarantor/Principal**] and managing member/general partner/manager of Borrower(s) and property manager (if an affiliate) is a [**limited liability company/partnership/corporation**] duly organized, validly existing and in good standing under the laws of the state of its formation.

2. Borrower, and (if required by state law) its managing member/general partner/manager is qualified to transact business in the state where its property is located.

3. The Loan Documents (a) have been properly authorized, executed, and delivered by or on behalf of Borrower, [**Guarantor/Principal**], managing member/general partner/manager of Borrower(s) (as applicable) and property manager (if an affiliate) as the case may be, and (b) constitute the legal, valid, and binding obligations of Borrower, [**Guarantor/Principal**], managing member/general partner/manager of Borrower(s) (as applicable) and property manager (if an affiliate) as the case may be, and are enforceable against each such party in accordance with their respective terms. [**General Partner/Managing Member/Manager**] is the sole [**General Partner/Managing Member/Manager**] of Borrower(s) and has been duly authorized by all necessary action to execute and deliver the Loan Documents on behalf of Borrower.

4. Borrower has the full power and authority to own and operate the Property and Improvements as presently conducted and as proposed to be conducted in connection with and following the consummation of the transactions described in the Loan Documents. Borrower is a single purpose entity and is engaged only in the business of owning and operating its Property and Improvements.

5. No approvals, consents, orders or authorizations of, or filings or registrations with, any governmental or regulatory authority or agency or any political subdivision or any court are necessary for the execution and delivery by Borrower, [**Guarantor/Principal**], managing member/general partner/manager of Borrower(s) (as applicable) and property manager (if an affiliate) of the Loan Documents or for the validity or the enforceability thereof, except for the recording or filing of the deed of trust or mortgage, as applicable, in the county where the Property is located and the appropriate UCC financing statements in the county where the Property is located and with the Secretary of State of the State of Borrower's formation.

6. The [**members**] [**shareholder**] [**partners**] of Borrower and [**Guarantor/Principal**], [**managing member/general partner/manager**] of Borrower (as applicable) and property manager (if an affiliate) have taken all actions necessary to authorize the execution, delivery and performance of the Loan Documents. Such execution, delivery and performance will not (a) conflict with, or result in a breach of the operating agreement or articles of organization of Borrower, [**Guarantor/Principal**], [**managing member/general partner/manager**] of Borrower (as applicable) or property manager (if an affiliate); (b) result in a violation of any applicable law, statute, ordinance or regulation, or to our knowledge, result in a violation of (i) any judgment, order, writ, injunction,

decree, or rule of any court, administrative agency, or other governmental authority or (ii) any determination or award of any arbitrator; (c) conflict with, constitute (with or without notice or lapse of time or both) a default under, result in a breach of or a violation of any term or provision of any material agreement or instrument to which Borrower, [**Guarantor/Principal**], [**managing member/general partner/manager**] of Borrower (as applicable) or property manager (if an affiliate) is a party or by which any of them is bound or by which any of their respective properties or assets are bound; or (d) to counsel's knowledge, result in the creation of any lien, charge or encumbrance on any property or assets of Borrower or [**Guarantor/Principal**], as the case may be, except as contemplated by the Loan Documents. Such execution, delivery, and performance will not constitute grounds for acceleration of the maturity of any material contractual obligation to which Borrower or [**Guarantor/Principal**] is a party or by which it may be bound.

7.  The UCC financing statements are in sufficient form for recording in the County Records of the county where each property is located and for filing in the Office of the Secretary of State of the state of each Borrower's formation. When each said UCC financing statement is filed in such Records and Offices, the security interest in the portion of the Property constituting Personal Property granted by Borrower to Lender under the Mortgages, and in which a security interest may be perfected by the filing of financing statements in the county where each property is located, will constitute fully perfected security interests in all right, title and interest of Borrower in said Personal Property.

8.  The filing of the UCC financing statements in the County Records of the county where Borrower's property is located and with the Secretary of State of the state of Borrower's formation are the only filings necessary to perfect the security interest in the personal property covered by Article 9 of the applicable state Uniform Commercial Code as described in the Financing Statements (the "**Personal Property**") which is owned by Borrower(s) on the date hereof, located in the county where Borrower's property is located and in which a security interest may be perfected by the filing of financing statements in the state of Borrower's formation.

9.  The provisions of the Mortgages create a valid lien in favor of Lender on the "**Property**" (as defined in the Mortgages) and the Mortgages are in sufficient form for recording in the County Records of the county where each property is located. The provisions of the Mortgages create a valid lien in favor of Lender on the "**Leases**" and "**Rents**."

10. To counsel's knowledge, there is no action, suit, proceeding, governmental investigation or arbitration, at law or equity, or before or by any governmental authority, pending or threatened against Borrower, [**Guarantor/Principal**], managing member/general partner/manager of Borrowers or property manager (if an affiliate) which will (a) result in a material adverse effect on Borrower, [**Guarantor/Principal**], or property manager (if an affiliate), or (b) materially or adversely affect the ability of Borrower, [**Guarantor/Principal**], or property manager (if an affiliate) to perform its respective obligations under the Loan Documents to which it is a party.

11. To counsel's knowledge, none of Borrower, [**Guarantor/Principal**], managing member/general partner/manager of Borrower or property manager (if an affiliate) is (a) in violation of any legal requirement which has or could reasonably be anticipated to have a material adverse effect on it or (b) subject to or in default with respect to any court order which would have a material adverse effect on it.

12. Under the laws of the state where the property is located, the Loan, including the interest reserved in the Note and all fees and charges paid or payable by or on behalf of Borrower or received or receivable by Lender, is not usurious or violative of any law or regulation governing the payment or receipt of interest.

13. The Loan and the Loan Documents are intended by their terms to be governed by the laws of the State of _____, except that creation, perfection, and enforcement of the liens granted in the mortgage or deed of trust, as applicable, are intended by their terms to be governed by the law of the state where the Property is located. Based upon the facts and circumstances of the transactions contemplated by the Loan Documents, a state court located in the state where the Property is located (or federal court applying the conflict of laws rules of the state where the Property is located) will give effect to the provisions of the Loan Documents that state that such Loan Documents are to be governed by and construed and interpreted in accordance with the laws of the State of _____ (except for matters of procedure and as required by mandatory provisions of the law of the state where the Property is located governing the creation, perfection, priority or enforcement of remedies with respect to any liens on the collateral described in the mortgage or deed of trust.

14. Borrower and property manager have been issued all licenses, permits, and approvals required by applicable governmental agencies for the operation of the Property as an [**independent/assisted living facility/skilled nursing facility**] and none of them are in violation of any such licenses, permits, or approvals.

# Appendix D

## Sample Asset-Based
## Opinion of Counsel

1. Borrower is a _____ which has been duly formed and organized and is validly existing and in good standing as a limited liability company under the laws of the [State] [Country] of _____ and is in good standing and authorized to transact business in _____.

2. Borrower has corporate requisite power and authority under its operating agreement and articles of organization to execute, deliver, and perform its obligations under the Loan Documents and to carry on its business as it is currently being conducted and as proposed to be conducted in connection with and following the consummation of the transactions described in the Loan Documents.

3. Borrower has been duly authorized by all necessary action to execute, deliver, perform, and observe its obligations under the Loan Documents to which it is a party (including passage of any necessary membership/shareholder or Board of Managers/Board of Directors consent).

4. _____ (i) is the _____ of Borrower, (ii) has been duly authorized by all necessary action to execute, deliver, perform, and observe its obligations under Borrower's operating agreement (including passage of any necessary resolutions or consents); and (iii) has been duly authorized by all necessary action to execute and deliver the Loan Documents on behalf of Borrower.

5. The Loan Documents have been duly authorized, executed (and acknowledged where necessary) and delivered to Lender, and all other necessary actions have been taken, so that the Loan Documents constitute the legal, valid and binding obligations of Borrower, enforceable against Borrower, in accordance with their respective terms. Observance by Borrower to the terms of the Loan Documents will not violate any federal or state rule or regulation applicable to Borrower.

6. Neither the execution and delivery of the Loan Documents nor the payment of the indebtedness evidenced by the Loan Documents nor the performance of the obligations and agreements contained in the Loan Documents will (a) conflict with, constitute an event of default under, or result in a breach of or a violation of the provisions of Borrower; (b) result in a violation of any applicable law, statute, ordinance, or regulation, or, to our knowledge, any judgment, order, writ injunction, decree, or rule of any court or other governmental agency or authority or of any determination or award of any arbitrator, or subject Borrower to any fine, penalty, or similar sanctions under any law or regulation; (c) to our knowledge, conflict with, constitute an event of default under, or result in a breach of or a violation of the provisions of any agreement or other instrument to which Borrower is a party or by which its property or assets are bound; or (d) to counsel's knowledge, result in the creation of any lien or encumbrance on any property of Borrower except as contemplated and permitted by the Loan Documents. Such execution, delivery, and performance will not constitute grounds for acceleration of the maturity of any material contractual obligation to which Borrower is bound.

7. To counsel's knowledge, there is no action, suit, proceeding, governmental investigation or arbitration, at law or in equity, or before any governmental authority, pending or threatened against or affecting Borrower, which if determined adversely to Borrower, would (i) have an adverse effect upon the priority or enforceability of Lender's rights under the Loan Documents, (ii) materially adversely affect the ability of Borrower to perform its obligations under the Loan Documents, or (iii) materially adversely affect Borrower.

8. To counsel's knowledge, Borrower is not (a) in violation of any legal requirement which has or could reasonably be anticipated to have a material adverse effect on Borrower, or (b) subject to or in default with respect to any court order which would have a material adverse effect on Borrower.

9. The amounts received or to be received by Lender under the Notes and other Loan Documents, including fees, charges, benefits, and other compensation, do not constitute usurious or otherwise unlawful interest and the Loan is not illegal under any applicable law or regulation.

10. No authorization, consent or approval of, or filings or registrations with or other action by any court, federal or state regulatory or governmental authority or other person or entity which has not been obtained or taken is required for the execution, delivery, validity, enforceability and/or performance by Borrower of any of the Loan Documents.

11. The Financing Statements are in form sufficient to create and perfect a lien on the Collateral.

12. Upon the filing of the Financing Statements in the State of _____ and payment of any applicable filing fees, all actions necessary to provide constructive notice of the liens created by the Financing Statements will have been taken.

13. The only recordation and filing necessary to perfect the security interests created by the Financing Statements in which a security interest in the Collateral may be perfected by filing under the UCC are as set forth as follows:

    13.1 The Financing Statements must be filed in the office of the Secretary of State for the State of _____.

    13.2 Except for filing of UCC continuation statements under the UCC relating to the Financing Statements, which UCC continuation statements must be filed in the same offices as were the original Financing Statements within the six-month period prior to each fifth anniversary of the original filing or recording date of each such statement in order to continue the perfection of the security interests described therein it is not necessary to re-record, re-register or re-file Financing Statements or to record, register or file any other or additional documents, instruments or statements in order to maintain the priority of the liens and security interests created thereby, *provided, however*, that (i) additional financing statements and fixture filings may be required to be filed if Borrower changes its name, identity or structure or state of organization and (ii) in the case of non-identifiable cash proceeds or non-cash proceeds of the Collateral, the security interest therein will be automatically perfected for a period of twenty days after they are received by the Borrower and otherwise will only be perfected if and to the extent that the Lender takes the steps required to obtain or maintain such perfection under UCC § 9-315.

14. The Loan and the Loan Documents are intended by their terms to be governed by the laws of the State of _____, except that creation, perfection and priority of liens and enforcement of remedies with respect to collateral described in the Loan Documents are intended by their terms to be governed by the law of the jurisdiction where each Borrower is incorporated (with respect to the security interest granted to Lender by such particular Borrower). Based upon the facts and circumstances of the transactions contemplated by the Loan Agreement, an _____ state court (or federal court applying _____ conflict of laws rules) will give effect to the provisions of the Loan Documents that state that such Loan Documents are to be governed by and construed and interpreted in accordance with the laws of the State of _____, except for matters of procedure and as required by mandatory provisions of _____ law governing the creation, perfection or priority of liens or enforcement of remedies with respect to any of the collateral described in the Loan Documents.

15. Borrower has been issued all licenses, permits and approvals required by applicable governmental agencies for operation as a _____, and Borrower is not in violation of any such licenses, permits or approvals.

16. The Note is secured by and entitled to the benefits and security of the Loan Documents. The Loan Documents contain customary and enforceable provisions to render the rights and remedies of the holder thereof adequate for the realization of the benefits of the security intended to be provided thereby, including realization by judicial or non-judicial foreclosure.

17. No fees, taxes or other charges, including, without limitation, intangible, documentary, stamp, recording taxes or similar charges are payable to the State of _____ or to any jurisdiction therein solely on account of the creation of the indebtedness evidenced or secured by the Loan Documents, the creation of the liens and security interests thereunder, or the filing, recording or registration of any other Loan Documents, except for insubstantial filing or recording fees, if any.

# Appendix E

## Example Representations and Warranties
## for Life Science Companies

### *Defined Terms*

**DEA** means the Drug Enforcement Administration of the United States of America and any successor agency thereof.

**Device Application** means a 510(k) premarket notification or premarket approval (PMA) application, as appropriate, as those terms are defined in the FDCA.

**Drug Application** means a new drug application, an abbreviated drug application, or a product license application for any Product, as appropriate, as those terms are defined in the FDCA.

**FDA** means the Food and Drug Administration of the United States of America or any successor entity thereto.

**FDCA** means the Federal Food, Drug, and Cosmetic Act, as amended, 21 U.S.C. Section 301 *et seq.* and all regulations promulgated thereunder, including but not limited to, 21 C.F.R. Parts 803, 806, 807, 812, and 820.

**Good Manufacturing Practices** means current good manufacturing practices, as set forth in the Quality System Regulation, 21 C.F.R. Part 820 and as set forth in 21 C.F.R. Parts 210 and 211.

**Healthcare Laws** means all applicable Laws relating to the Products, private label and other drug distributions, and the possession, control, warehousing, marketing, sale and distribution of medical devices and/or pharmaceuticals, including, without limitation, all federal and state laws governing the sale and distribution of drugs, including over-the-counter drugs, biologicals and supplements, including the Controlled Substances Act (21 U.S.C. §§ 801 *et seq.*), the Food, Drug and Cosmetic Act of 1938 (21 U.S.C. Chapter 9), the Dietary Supplement Health and Education Act (P.L. 103-417 (1994)) and the Omnibus Budget and Reconciliation Act of 1990 (P.L. 101-508 (1990)), and also the Generic Drug Enforcement Act of 1992.

**Permits** means registrations, listing, licenses, certificates, accreditations (including ISO 13485 or ISO 13488), product clearances or approvals, provider numbers or provider authorizations, marketing authorizations, other authorizations, registrations, permits, consents and approvals or exemptions thereto required in connection with the conduct of Borrower's business or to comply with any applicable laws, including, without limitation, Healthcare Laws, establishment registrations, establishment licenses, device listings, drug listings, drug establishment registrations, Investigational Device Exemptions (IDEs), 510(k) exemptions, 510(k) clearances, PMA approvals, Drug Identification Numbers (DINs), as those terms are defined in the FDCA and implementing regulations and the corresponding medical devices regulations and food and drug regulations, and those issued by State governments for the conduct of Borrower's business or necessary in the manufacturing, importing, exporting, possession, ownership, warehousing, marketing, promoting, sale, labeling, furnishing, distribution or delivery of goods or services under laws applicable to the business of Borrower or any Device Application or Drug Application.

**Products** means any products manufactured, sold, licensed, developed, tested, or marketed by Borrower.

**Recall** means the removal, modification, relabeling, destruction or correction of a marketed product that the FDA considers to be in violation of the laws it administers and against which the FDA would initiate legal action.

1. Borrower hereby represents and warrants to Lender that Borrower:

   a. has obtained all Permits, or has contracted with third parties holding Permits, necessary for compliance with all laws, including Healthcare Laws and the FDCA, and for the research, development, testing, manufacturing, packaging, labeling, handling, storage, advertising, promoting, marketing, distribution, and communication of the Products, and all such Permits are current;

   b. has been operating in compliance with all Healthcare Laws, including but not limited to, reporting to FDA of device malfunctions and/or device-related serious injuries or deaths pursuant to 21 C.F.R. § 803 and reporting to FDA of corrections or removals pursuant to 21 C.F.R. § 806;

   c. has not received any written notice that any governmental authority including, without limitation, the FDA, the Office of the Inspector General of HHS, or the United States Department of Justice has commenced or threatened to initiate any action against Borrower, any action to enjoin Borrower or its officers, directors, employees, shareholders or their agents and affiliates, from conducting their businesses at any facility owned or used by them or for any material civil penalty, injunction, seizure or criminal action;

   d. except as set forth on **Schedule** ___, has not received from the FDA at any time since _____, 20___, a warning letter, Form FDA-483, "Untitled Letter," other correspondence or notice setting forth allegedly objectionable observations or alleged violations of laws and regulations enforced by the FDA or DEA, including but not limited to the FDCA, or any comparable correspondence from any state or local authority responsible for regulating medical device products, drug products and establishments, or any comparable correspondence from any foreign counterpart of the FDA or DEA, or any comparable correspondence from any foreign counterpart of any state or local authority with regard to any Product or the manufacture, processing, packing, or holding thereof; and

   e. except as set forth on **Schedule** ___, has not engaged in any Recalls or other forms of product retrieval from the marketplace of any Products since _____, 20___.

2. With respect to Products:

    a. All Products are listed on **Exhibit \_\_\_** and Borrower has delivered to Lender on or prior to the Closing Date all Permits relating to such Products; *provided, however*, that, if after the Closing Date, Borrower wishes to manufacture, sell, develop, test or market any new Product, Borrower shall give prior written notice to Lender of such intention and *further, provided,* that, if Borrower shall at any time obtain any new or additional Permits from the FDA, DEA or parallel state or local authorities, or foreign counterparts of the FDA, DEA or parallel state or local authorities, with respect to any Product which has previously been disclosed to Lender, Borrower shall promptly give written notice to Lender of such new or additional Permits, along with a copy thereof);

    b. Each Product is not adulterated or misbranded within the meaning of the FDCA;

    c. Each Product is not an article prohibited from introduction into interstate commerce under the provisions of the FDCA;

    d. Each Product has been and/or shall be manufactured, labeled, imported, possessed, owned, warehoused, marketed, promoted, sold, labeled, furnished, distributed and marketed in accordance with all applicable Permits and Healthcare Laws, including but not limited to the FDCA;

    e. Each Product has been and/or shall be designed and manufactured in accordance with Good Manufacturing Practices;

    f. With respect to any Product being tested or manufactured by Borrower, Borrower has received and shall be in compliance with, and such Product shall be the subject of, all Permits needed in connection with the testing or manufacture of such Product as such testing is currently being conducted by or on behalf of Borrower, and Borrower has not received any notice from any applicable government authority, specifically including the FDA, that such government authority is conducting an investigation or review of (A) Borrower's manufacturing facilities and processes for such Product which have disclosed any material deficiencies or violations of laws (including Healthcare laws) and/or the Permits related to the manufacture of such Product, or (B) any such Permit or that any such Permit has been revoked or withdrawn, nor has any such governmental authority issued any order or recommendation stating that the development, testing and/or manufacturing of such Product by Borrower should cease;

    g. With respect to any Product marketed or sold by Borrower, Borrower shall have received, and such Product shall be the subject of, all Permits needed in connection with the marketing and sales of such Product as currently being marketed or sold by Borrower, and Borrower has not received any notice from any applicable governmental authority, specifically including the FDA, that such governmental authority is conducting an investigation or review of any such Permit or approval or that any such Permit has been revoked or withdrawn, nor has any such governmental authority issued any order or recommendation stating that such marketing or sales of such Product cease or that such Product be recalled from the marketplace;

h. Each Product that is not a "new drug", as that term is defined in 21 U.S.C. Section 321(p), is generally recognized by qualified experts as safe and effective for its intended uses as those terms have been interpreted by FDA and the United States Supreme Court; and

i. Each Product for which a Drug Efficacy Study Implementation (DESI) Notice has been published in the Federal Register and each Product that is identical to, related to, or similar to such a drug conforms with the requirements set forth in such DESI Notice.

3. In connection with the research, development, testing, manufacture, processing, handling, packaging, labeling, storage, advertising, promoting, marketing or sale of each and any Product by Borrower, Borrower shall comply fully and completely in all respects with all NDAs, ANDAs, all Healthcare Laws and all applicable laws including, but not limited to, the FDA Act, the Prescription Drug Marketing Act of 1987, as amended from time to time, Generic Drug Enforcement Act of 1992, as amended from time to time, and the Controlled Substances Act, as amended from time to time, the United States Code, Title 21, and the Code of Federal Regulations, Title 21, and Permits at all times issued by any government authority, specifically including the FDA, with respect to such development, testing, manufacture, marketing or sales of such Product by Borrower as such activities are at any such time being conducted by Borrower.

4. Neither Borrower nor any of its affiliates, directors, members, employees, agents, officers or managers:

a. has been convicted of or charged with any violation of any law related to any Federal Health Care Programs, as defined in 42 U.S.C. § 1320a-7b(f);

b. has been convicted of any crime or engaged in any conduct for which debarment is mandated by 21 U.S.C. Section 335a(a) or authorized by 21 U.S.C. Section 335a(b);

c. has made an untrue statement of material fact or fraudulent statement to the FDA or failed to disclose a material fact required to be disclosed to the FDA, committed an act, made a statement, or failed to make a statement that could reasonably be expected to provide a basis for the FDA to invoke its policy respecting "Fraud, Untrue Statements of Material Facts, Bribery, and Illegal Gratuities," set forth in 56 Fed. Regulation 46191 (September 10, 1991);

d. has been convicted of, charged with, or investigated for any violation of law related to fraud, theft, embezzlement, breach of fiduciary responsibility, financial misconduct, obstruction of an investigation, or controlled substances; or

e. has been excluded, suspended or debarred from participation, or are otherwise ineligible to participate, in (i) any Federal Health Care Programs, or in Federal procurement or non procurement programs or (ii) any other federal or state government programs or activities, including, without limitation, the FDA, or (iii) have committed any violation of law that is reasonably expected to serve as the basis for any such exclusion, suspension, debarment or other ineligibility.

5.  Borrower is in compliance with (a) the Federal Health Care Program requirements applicable to Borrower, and (b) federal and state reporting obligations applicable to Borrower, including, without limitation, any state law reporting obligations relating to sales and marketing to healthcare professionals, any price reporting obligations pursuant to the Medicaid Drug Rebate program, the Medicare program, and any other federal or state programs (including, without limitation, the 340B Drug Pricing program).

6.  Neither Borrower nor any officer, manager, director, employee or agent of Borrower, nor any other person or entity acting on behalf of Borrower, acting alone or together, have directly or indirectly (i) made any illegal or unethical contribution, gift, bribe, rebate, payoff, commissions, promotional allowances, influence payment, kickback, or other payment or economic benefit to any person or entity, private or public, regardless of what form, whether in money, property, or services; (ii) established or maintained any fund or asset that has not been recorded in the books and records of Borrower, (iii) engaged in any business practices or conducted any dealings that are materially contrary to accepted industry standards; or (iv) aided, abetted, caused (directly or indirectly), participated in, or otherwise conspired with, any person or entity to violate the terms of any judgment, sentence, order or decree of any court or governmental authority.

# Appendix F

## Example Representations and Warranties
## for Healthcare Facilities

### *Defined Terms*

**CON** means any certificate of need or similar license which determines that there is a need for a healthcare facility at a particular location or within a certain geographic region.

**Healthcare Laws** means all applicable laws relating to the possession, control, warehousing, marketing, sale and distribution of pharmaceuticals, the operation of medical or senior housing facilities (such as, but not limited to, nursing homes, skilled nursing facilities, rehabilitation hospitals, intermediate care facilities and adult care facilities), patient healthcare, patient healthcare information, patient abuse, the quality and adequacy of medical care, rate setting, equipment, personnel, operating policies, fee splitting, including, without limitation, (a) all federal and state fraud and abuse laws, including, without limitation, the federal Anti-Kickback Statute (42 U.S.C. § 1320a-7b(6)), the Stark Law (42 U.S.C. § 1395nn), the civil False Claims Act (31 U.S.C. §§ 3729 *et seq.*), (b) TRICARE, (c) HIPAA, (d) Medicare, (e) Medicaid, (f) quality, safety and accreditation standards and requirements of all applicable state laws or regulatory bodies, (g) all laws, policies, procedures, requirements and regulations pursuant to which Permits are issued, and (h) any and all other applicable healthcare laws, regulations, manual provisions, policies and administrative guidance, each as may be amended from time to time.

**HIPAA** means the Health Insurance Portability and Accountability Act of 1996, as the same may be amended, modified or supplemented from time to time, and any successor statute thereto, and any and all rules or regulations promulgated from time to time thereunder.

**HIPAA Compliant** shall mean that the applicable person or entity is in compliance with each of the applicable requirements of HIPAA, and is not and could not reasonably be expected to become the subject of any civil or criminal penalty, process, claim, action or proceeding, or any administrative or other regulatory review, survey, process or proceeding (other than routine surveys or reviews conducted by any government health plan or other accreditation entity) that could result in any of the foregoing or that could reasonably be expected to adversely affect such person's or entity's business, operations, assets, properties or condition (financial or otherwise), in connection with any actual or potential violation by such Person of the provisions of HIPAA.

**Medicaid** means the medical assistance programs administered by state agencies and approved pursuant to the terms of Title XIX of the Social Security Act, codified at 42 U.S.C. §§ 1396 *et seq.*

**Medicare** means the program of health benefits for the aged and disabled administered pursuant to the terms of Title XVIII of the Social Security Act, codified at 42 U.S.C. §§ 1395 *et seq.*

**Permit** means all governmental licenses, authorizations, provider numbers, supplier numbers, registrations, permits, certificates, franchises, qualifications, accreditations, consents and approvals required under all applicable laws and required in order to carry on its business as now conducted, including as issued or required under Healthcare Laws applicable to the business of Borrower or necessary in the possession, ownership, warehousing, marketing, promoting, sale, labeling, furnishing, distribution or delivery of goods or services under Healthcare Laws applicable to the business of Borrower.

**Project** means any facility from which Borrower provides or furnishes goods or services, including, without limitation, any hospital, skilled nursing facility, assisted living facility, independent living facility or similar facility, and includes, without limitation, any business location of Borrower which is subject to any Permit.

**Resident Agreements** means the singular or collective reference to all patient and resident care agreements, admission agreements and service agreements which include an occupancy agreement and all amendments, modifications or supplements thereto.

**Third Party Payor** means Medicare, Medicaid, TRICARE, and other state or federal healthcare program, Blue Cross and/or Blue Shield, private insurers, managed care plans and any other Person or entity which presently or in the future maintains Third Party Payor Programs.

**Third Party Payor Programs** means all payment and reimbursement programs, sponsored by a Third Party Payor, in which Borrower participates.

**TRICARE** means the program administered pursuant to 10 U.S.C. Section 1071 *et. seq.*, Sections 1320a-7 and 1320a-7a of Title 42 of the United States Code, and the regulations promulgated pursuant to such statutes.

Borrower hereby represents and warrants to Lender as follows:

1. Borrower has obtained all Permits, material licenses, accreditations and approvals of governmental authorities and all other persons or entities necessary to own or lease and operate the Project or to otherwise provide healthcare services. Borrower is in material compliance with the terms and conditions of all Permits and all Permits are valid and in full force and effect. Borrower has no knowledge that any governmental authority is considering limiting, suspending or revoking any such Permit.

2. All of the payor agreements or payor accounts between Borrower and insurance carriers, self-insured employee trusts or other payors are currently in full force and effect. Borrower maintains Medicare and Medicaid provider status and is the holder of the provider identification numbers associated therewith, all of which are currently valid.

3. There are no outstanding deficiencies or work orders of any authority having jurisdiction over Borrower requiring conformity to any applicable statute, regulation, ordinance or law pertaining to Borrower or its facilities in general, including but not limited to the Third Party Payor Programs. No Project is currently subject to any plan of correction that has not been accepted by or is currently the subject of a review by the applicable state authority. All Medicare, Medicaid, and private insurance cost reports and financial reports submitted by Borrower are and will be materially accurate and complete and have not been and will not be misleading in any

material respects. No cost reports for the Project remains "open" or unsettled and there are no current, pending or outstanding Medicare, Medicaid or other Third Party Payor Program reimbursement audits or appeals pending with respect to the Project or Borrower, except in accordance with applicable settlement or appeals procedures that are timely and diligently pursued (provided that the aggregate amount at issue in any appeals does not exceed $25,000) and except as a result of any processing delays of the applicable Third Party Payor Program.

4. Borrower is not subject to any proceeding, suit or, to Borrower's knowledge, investigation by any federal, state or local government or quasi-governmental body, agency, board or authority or any other administrative or investigative body (including the Office of the Inspector General of the United States Department of Health and Human Services): (i) which may result in the imposition of a fine, sanction, a lower reimbursement rate for services rendered to eligible patients, or which would have a material adverse effect on any Borrower or its operations; (ii) which could result in the revocation, transfer, surrender, suspension or other impairment of any provider agreement or Permit; (iii) which pertains to or requests any voluntary disclosure pertaining to a potential overpayment matter involving the submission of claims to such payor by Borrower; (iv) which pertains to any state or federal Medicare or Medicaid cost reports or claims filed by Borrower; or (v) which requires Borrower to rework or redesign the Project or to provide additional furniture, fixtures, equipment or inventory so as to conform to or comply with any existing law, code or standard.

5. All billing practices of Borrower, including those with respect to all Third Party Payors, including the Third Party Payor Programs, if applicable, and private insurance companies, including managed care organizations, have been and will be in compliance with all applicable laws, regulations and policies of such Third Party Payors and Third Party Payor Programs in all material respects. Borrower has not made any decision not to renew any participation agreement or provider agreement or other Permit, nor is there any action pending or threatened to impose material intermediate or alternative sanctions with respect to the Project.

6. Neither Borrower nor any of its affiliates or any of their officers, directors, agents or employees, nor any agent acting on behalf of or for the benefit of any of the foregoing, has directly or indirectly in connection with Borrower or otherwise: (i) offered or paid any remuneration, in cash or in kind to any past or present suppliers, patients, medical provider members, contractors or Third Party Payors in violation of applicable law; (ii) given or agreed to give, or is aware that there has been made or that there is any agreement to make, any gift or gratuitous payment of any kind, nature or description (whether in money, property or services) to any customer or potential customer, supplier or potential supplier, contractor, third party payor or any other person in violation of applicable law; (iii) made or agreed to make, or is aware that there has been made or that there is any agreement to make, any contribution, payment of gift of funds or property to, or for the private use of, any governmental official, employee or agent where either the contribution, payment or gift or the purpose of such contribution, payment or gift is or was illegal under applicable law; or (iv) made, or agreed to make, or is aware that there has been made or that there is any agreement to make, any payment to any person with the intention or understanding that any part of such payment would be used for any purpose other than that described in the documents supporting such payment.

7. Neither Borrower nor any of its affiliates or any of their officers, directors, agents or employees, is a party to any contract, lease agreement or other arrangement (including any joint venture or consulting agreement) related to Borrower with any physician, healthcare facility, hospital, nursing facility, home health agency or other person who is in a position to make or influence referrals to or otherwise generate business or operations for Borrower to provide services, lease space, lease equipment or engage in any other venture or activity that is prohibited by law or that did not provide commercially reasonable terms and fair market value consideration for the goods, property, services or use of money provided, exchanged or acquired thereunder at the time entered into.

8. Borrower is in compliance with the applicable provisions of 42 U.S.C. § 1320a-7b prohibiting illegal remuneration (including kickbacks, bribes, or rebates) by properly disclosing and appropriately reflecting its pricing in any cost claimed or charge made, if any, under the Third Party Payor Programs.

9. Borrower has not granted to any third party the right to reduce the number of licensed beds, persons served or units in the Project or the right to apply for approval to move any and all of the licensed beds, persons served or units in the Project to any other location and there are no proceedings or contemplated to reduce the number of licensed beds, persons served or units in the Project.

10. All Resident Agreements comply with all applicable Healthcare Laws. Without the prior written consent of Lender, Borrower shall not: (i) modify the form of Resident Agreement approved by Lender; (ii) accept any payment under any Resident Agreement in violation of the cash management or lockbox provisions required by lender; or (iii) enter into any Resident Agreement upon rates other than market rates or upon a form that fails to comply with applicable Laws.

11. Borrower is in compliance with all applicable Healthcare Laws. Borrower is HIPAA Compliant.

12. If required, Borrower has and shall maintain in full force and effect a valid CON for no less than the number of beds and units in the Project. Borrower shall maintain any applicable CON free from restrictions or known conflicts which would materially impair the use or operation of the Project for its current use, and shall not permit any CON to become provisional, probationary, or restricted in any way.

# Index

Healthcare Finance: A Primer, First Edition

# Notes

# Notes

# Notes

# Notes

# Notes